CENTRE POMPIDOU

THE NATIONAL MUSEUM OF MODERN ART

PAINTINGS AND SCULPTURES

Jacinto Lageira

Centre
Pompidou

EDITIONS
SCALA

The author would like to thank all those who have helped in the creation of this work, in particular Nathalie Leleu and Denys Riout.

Éditions Scala are grateful to Françoise Bertaux, publications manager of the Centre Pompidou, for her efficiency and readiness to help, France Sabary of the museum's photographic archive, and Evelyne Pomey of the documentation department.

The exhibition areas of the historical collections of the National Museum of Modern Art were refurbished with the support of Pierre Bergé, Yves Saint Laurent and the YⱯeⱾⱯIN₸ⱠAURENT Company.

Graphic design:
★ Bronx (Paris)

Cover design:
Jean-Pierre Jauneau

Layout:
Thierry Renard

Translation:
Simon Knight

Copy-editing:
Bernard Wooding

Diffusion - Distribution:
CDE - Sodis

It is possible that the works presented in this book will not be on show when you visit the National Museum of Modern Art. This is because the museum's curators change the displays on a regular basis so that they can present the largest number of works and artists as possible.

CONTENTS

Foreword

The ever-expanding collection of the National Museum of Modern Art represents a veritable anthology of the various artistic forms of the twentieth century. It offers, at the heart of the Centre Georges Pompidou, an exceptional tour of the field, one that is regularly renewed by new hangings and enriched with new acquisitions. Some of the major figures of modern art are particularly well represented, such as Matisse, Picasso, Brancusi, Delaunay, Kandinsky, Léger, Rouault and many others who, thanks to gifts or bequests, as well as acquisition and donations, have become beacons lighting our way.

But the strength of this collection lies in the way that it embraces so many different disciplines: photography, graphic art, new media, experimental film, architecture, and design. From these intersections and interactions are born other artistic approaches, including the most recent tendencies in contemporary art, to which the museum devotes much space.

Museum of modern art, museum of contemporary art, museum of every discipline – such is National Museum of Modern Art today, nearly half a century after it was created, in this unique cultural institution that is the Centre Georges Pompidou.

Alfred Pacquement
Director of the MNAM/CCI

<
View of the west terrace,
Max Ernst
The Big Turtle
and *The Big Frog*
1967-1974

The MNAM Collection Today

Now numbering some forty-five thousand works or items, the MNAM collections have been built up by stratification, accumulation and the interaction of various social and historical factors over a relatively short period of time. Barely half a century has passed since the National Museum of Modern Art was opened (at the Palais de Tokyo) in 1947. Though short, the museum's history has been eventful, including a change in venue in 1977, when the collections were moved to the Pompidou Centre. During the time it has been housed at the Centre, the museum was first restructured in 1986, to plans drawn up by Gae Aulenti.

Today, after a closure of two years during which the Pompidou Centre was completely refurbished, the permanent collection is displayed in accordance with a new, multi-disciplinary approach in exhibition areas enlarged and remodelled by the architect Jean-François Bodin. It now occupies two complete floors (fourteen thousand square metres, as against ten thousand previously) and features a selection of one thousand five hundred works covering all aspects of the visual arts in the 20th century (painting, sculpture, drawing, photography, the cinema and video). It also illustrates the links between these disciplines and architecture and contemporary design – two fields which came within the remit of the MNAM in 1992, when the museum merged with the Centre de Création Industrielle.

A look back over the history of the museum reveals that the collections were formed in three main stages, which roughly correspond with the three main methods of acquisition: donations and bequests, purchases, and donations in lieu of tax.

The Major Donations

During the first twenty years of its life, the MNAM's budget was relatively modest, only occasionally allowing the museum to purchase really important works. There were, however, a few exceptions: Francis Picabia's *Udnie* in 1949, Constantin Brancusi's *Le Coq* (*The Cockerel*) in 1947, Juan Gris's *Le Petit Déjeuner* (*The Breakfast*) also in 1947, and Picasso's stage curtain for *Parade* in 1955.

But most new acquisitions during this period were the result of donations or bequests, made possible by the generosity of artists and their families, and collectors and friends of the museum. Another important factor was the hard work of Jean Cassou, director of the MNAM at this time, who over many years had built up close and friendly relationships with the French art circles concerned.

These donations, especially those made by the artists themselves or their friends and families, provided the collection's real foundation, in the full sense of the word. They gave it its historical basis, and also its particular personality, which differs from that of comparable collections in other parts of the world. As far as the 20th century is concerned, neither the Tate Gallery in London nor the MOMA in New York owns groups of works of the same type: mini-collections which illustrate the entire career of an artist through studies, drawings and documentation (in addition to major works), virtually providing the material to reconstitute his or her studio.

It is not possible to mention all these donations, but the names include Picasso (eleven canvases, including the *Rocking-chair* [1943] in 1945), Chagall (seven paintings, including his *Double portrait au verre de vin* / *Double Portrait with Glass of Wine* [1917] in 1947) and Brancusi (who bequeathed the entire contents of his workshop in 1957), followed by Braque (1963), Laurens (1967), Rouault, Pevsner, Kupka, Gonzáles, Kandinsky and Delaunay among others.

The great collectors of the same generation also played their part. Special mention should be made of André Lefèvre in respect of Cubism, Raoul La Roche (four works by Braque), Baroness Gourgaud (*La Lecture* / *Reading* by Fernand Léger), Marie Cuttoli and Henri Laugier (who in 1963 donated a superb group of *papiers collés* by Picasso).

Thanks to these combined efforts, the collection began to take shape. By 1961 it already numbered over a thousand paintings and three hundred sculptures, but very few 'contemporary' works (i.e. from the 1950s) and almost nothing of American origin (the only exception being a sculpture by Calder).

A Targeted Purchasing Policy

In the 1970s, there was a growing awareness that the museum was falling behind in acquiring new works. While the project for the future Pompidou Centre was maturing, the state – at the instigation of President Pompidou, who was a connoisseur and admirer of modern and contemporary art – decided to become more involved and provide larger sums for purchasing new works. In 1975, the MNAM could rely for the first time on a substantial, independently managed budget, and the amount was doubled again in 1982.

Successive directors of the museum (Jean Leymarie from 1969 to 1973, Pontus Hulten from 1974 to 1981, Dominique Bozo from 1981 to 1986) were therefore able at last to embark on an ambitious purchasing policy, each with very definite objectives. Pontus Hulten's concern was to make up the deficiency in American art, Surrealism and international art generally. Dominique Bozo continued to consolidate and develop the Matisse, Miró, Giacometti, Dubuffet and Léger collections, concerned that France should retain essential aspects of its national heritage.

They played a very active role, and during this period many major works, including some outstanding masterpieces, were added to the historical collection. It would be tedious to list them all, but a few should be mentioned, in the order they were acquired: Derain, *Les Péniches / The Barges* [1906] in 1972; Dalí, *La Vache spectrale / The Spectral Cow* [1928] in 1974; de Chirico, *Portrait prémonitoire de Guillaume Apollinaire / Premonitory Portrait of Guillaume Apollinaire* [1914] in 1975; Matisse, *Le Violoniste à la fenêtre / Violinist at the Window* [1918] in 1975; Dubuffet, *Le Voyageur sans boussole / Traveller without a Compass* [1952] in 1976; Miró, *La Sieste / The Siesta* [1925] in 1977; Robert Delaunay, *Le Poète Philippe Soupault* [1922] in 1978; Giacometti, *Portrait de Jean Genet* [1955] in 1980; Kirchner, *Toilette* [1913] in 1980; Klee, *Rythmisches / Rhythmus* [1930] in 1984, to name but a few.

At the same time, part of the budget was reserved for major contemporary purchases (*The Big Five* by Jasper Johns, *Métamatic no. 1* by Tinguely, *Le Magasin / The Store* by Ben, groups of works by Yves Klein and Martial Raysse). American art, so long ignored in Paris, found its way into the collections as a result of solidarity with the Pompidou Centre in the United States. The new acquisitions included *Oracle* by Rauschenberg, *Shining Forth* by Barnett Newman, and *Ghost Drum Set* by Oldenburg.

While stressing acquisitions through purchase, we should of course not forget the continuing support of the museum's major donors, in particular the Menil and Scaler Foundations (e.g. Malevich, *Black Cross*), and the loyalty of artists' families (in 1976 Nina Kandinsky gave the MNAM fifteen paintings by Kandinsky, including *Improvisation III* [1909] and *Mit dem Schwarzen Bogen / With the Black Arch* [1912]; the Lipchitz Foundation donated thirty-five of the sculptor's original plaster casts; Mme Jean Matisse contributed Henri Matisse's coloured-paper cut-outs for the Chapelle du Rosaire in Vence; and Mme Ida Chagall presented five major canvases by her father). A final mention should go to the donation made by Louise and Michel Leiris in 1984, which at a stroke added almost two hundred works to the museum, and greatly enhanced its collection of Cubist art.

Donation in Lieu of Taxation

In 1968 the French government introduced a special measure to ensure that major works were retained for the national collections – an arrangement whereby the heirs of artists and collectors were allowed to donate works of art in lieu of inheritance tax, provided of course that such works were considered as being of vital interest to the national heritage. The benefits of this measure – in the case of 20th-century art – began to be felt in the early 1980s. As a result, the museum was able to acquire a large part of the estates of artists (Chagall, Derain, Giacometti, Magnelli, Vieira da Silva, Dubuffet) and dealers, together with enlightened amateurs (Pierre Matisse, Robert Lebel, Alfred Richet). It has also added masterpieces by Bonnard, Braque, Derain, Dubuffet, Duchamp, Giacometti, Klee, Laurens, Man Ray, Matisse and Miró to the historical collection.

Needless to say, the museum also continued to make purchases throughout this period, but these have become less frequent – as few as one or two a year – because of the spiralling prices being paid for sought-after works of art. It is worth mentioning the three-stage acquisition of *Bleu I, Bleu II* and *Bleu III* (1961) by Miró (in 1984, 1988 and 1993 respectively), Giacometti's *Femme égorgée / Woman with Her Throat Cut* (1932) in 1992, Fontana's *Concetto spaziale* (1949) in 1993, and Balthus's *Alice* (1933) in 1995.

The personal predilections of successive directors of the MNAM – Germain Viatte from 1993 to 1996 and Werner Spies from 1997 to 2000 – have of course influenced the acquisitions policy, as is evident, for example, from the purchases of works by Picabia, Dix, Schad and Oldenburg in recent years.

But there has also been a sustained determination to build up strong nuclei of contemporary works, representing Minimalism (based on Richard Serra), the Supports/Surfaces movement, Pop Art, Nouveau Réalisme, Arte Povera (of which the MNAM probably owns the best collection of any museum), Joseph Beuys, Gerhard Richter and so on. A special place has been accorded to large-scale installations and environments, from Dubuffet's *Jardin d'hiver / Winter Garden* (1970), to Beuys's *Plight* (1985) and Mike Kelley and Tony Oursler's video installation *The Poetic Project* (1977–97), donated in 1999 by the Friends of the museum.

Isabelle Monod-Fontaine
Assistant Director, MNAM

Emphasis on Colour
1905–1915: from the Fauves to the abstract movements

Because of the deep-rooted tradition of the image in Western art, painting was the focus of the first artistic revolutions of the early 20th century and the prime target of avant-garde artists.

Rules which had been systematised to the point of academic sterility by the end of the 19th century – in respect of copying, drawing, technique, modelling, perspective, the hierarchy of themes and genres – were brought crashing down. The aim was no longer to render the reality of the perceived world as faithfully as possible, but to leave more and more room for individual expression and to investigate the procedures and purposes of art itself. At the same time, artists began to develop some of the material possibilities of painting in terms of facture, technique and colour.

Colour had already been explored by the Impressionists, the Neo-Impressionists and the Symbolists, who had advocated its use in pure form, although this was not a rigid rule. With the Fauves, it became one of the formal elements which triggered profound changes in the aesthetics of painting. Indeed, it was because they used colours hitherto regarded as garish and violent that, at the Salon d'Automne in Paris in 1905, the artists exhibiting in room VII – who included Henri Matisse, André Derain and Maurice de Vlaminck – were nicknamed 'fauves' (wild beasts). A work characteristic of the Fauvist period, Derain's *Faubourg de Collioure* (*Outskirts of Collioure*) shows the importance accorded to sharp colour contrasts and clearly visible brushwork. Even more than was the case for van Gogh or Gauguin, colour was no longer used to fill previously drawn outlines but became – to use Derain's expression – 'a parallel drawing'. It is true that their figures did sometimes have outlines, and their use of pure colours was not systematic, but by giving greater autonomy to colour, and seeing it as an end in itself, the Fauves bade farewell to naturalism and the slavish copying of external reality. Trees might be blue or hair orange; three-dimensional perspective was discarded; artists left their work deliberately unfinished, often with the canvas showing between the brushstrokes; they insisted on impasto effects and arbitrary processes became an integral part of their work. But it was colour which dominated and became in a sense the subject of the painting. The resulting technique was more spontaneous, forms tended to dissolve, and the deeply rooted concept of painting as an imitation of perceived reality was replaced by the idea of the picture as an autonomous artefact, its constituent elements laid bare for all to see.

During the short period the Fauves remained together as a group (1905–8), and though they had no established programme or style, their use of colour primarily as paint on canvas – in other words detached from the actual colours of the people and things they were supposed to be imitating – served to affirm the artificial nature of painting. This approach was defended by the painter and critic Maurice Denis, who wrote as follows in *L'Ermitage* in 1905: 'But what is particularly evident in Matisse is artifice; not literary artifice, as in a quest for idealistic expression; nor decorative artifice, as in the work of Turkish and Persian carpet-weavers; no, it is something still more abstract; it is painting outside all contingency, painting as an end in itself, the act of painting.' The use of colour to compose forms and space led to a considerable simplification of the painter's resources, giving them greater impact by making them independent of the motif and therefore better able to emphasise optical sensation and the artist's inner expression. This is why, in 1908, Matisse wrote in the

>
André Derain
Chatou, 1880 –
Chambourcy, 1954
*Le Faubourg de Collioure
(Outskirts of Collioure)*
1905

Oil on canvas
59.5 x 73.2 cm
*Purchased 1966
AM 4367 P*

Grande Revue: 'The dominant tendency of colour should be to serve expression as best as possible . . . My choice of colours is not based on any scientific theory: it is based on observation, on feeling, on the experience of my sensitivity . . . All I do is seek to apply colours which render my sensations.'

While the Fauves were causing a scandal at the Salon d'Automne, an association of young German artists, Die Brücke (The Bridge), was being founded in Dresden (it was officially dissolved in 1913 in Berlin). Gathered around Ernst Ludwig Kirchner, who drafted the group's brief manifesto, the artists of the first Expressionist wave (Fritz Bleyl, Erich Heckel, Karl Schmidt-Rottluff) were interested in the same genres as the Fauves (landscapes, nudes, portraits, still lifes). Like the Fauves, they drew

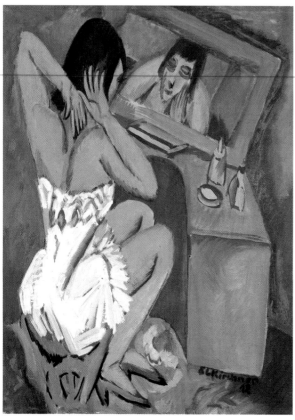

<
Ernst Ludwig Kirchner
Aschaffenburg, 1880 –
Frauenkirch, Davos, 1938
*Toilette – Frau vor
dem Spiegel*
*(Toilette – Woman
Before the Mirror)*
1912

Oil on canvas
100.5 x 75.5 cm
Purchased 1980
AM 1980-54

inspiration from African and Oceanic art, and also worked to renew the role of colour. However, they painted and sculpted with a brutality foreign to the Fauves, and their technique reflected the exuberant and disturbing quality of their work. They would sometimes dilute their paints with petrol, applying them with broad strokes of brush or palette knife, with the result that the canvas looked like an impasto mass thrown on at random. The artists of Die Brücke produced exaggerated deformations of their subject matter by sharply contrasting the figure with the background, creating distortions, and depicting faces and bodies as if they had been hewn with an axe. Despite the anguish or existential pain which seems to animate these angular figures with their clear, powerful lines (Kirchner, *Toilette*), the human being remained at the heart of Expressionist painting. As Kirchner himself affirmed: 'Art is made by man. His own person is the centre of all art, as his form and mass are the foundation and starting point of all sensation. That is why any teaching of the things of art must begin with man himself.'

>
Wassily Kandinsky
Moscow, 1866 –
Neuilly-sur-Seine, 1944
Mit dem schwarzen Bogen
(With the Black Arch)
1912

Oil on canvas
189 x 198 cm
Gift of Nina Kandinsky, 1976
AM 1976-852

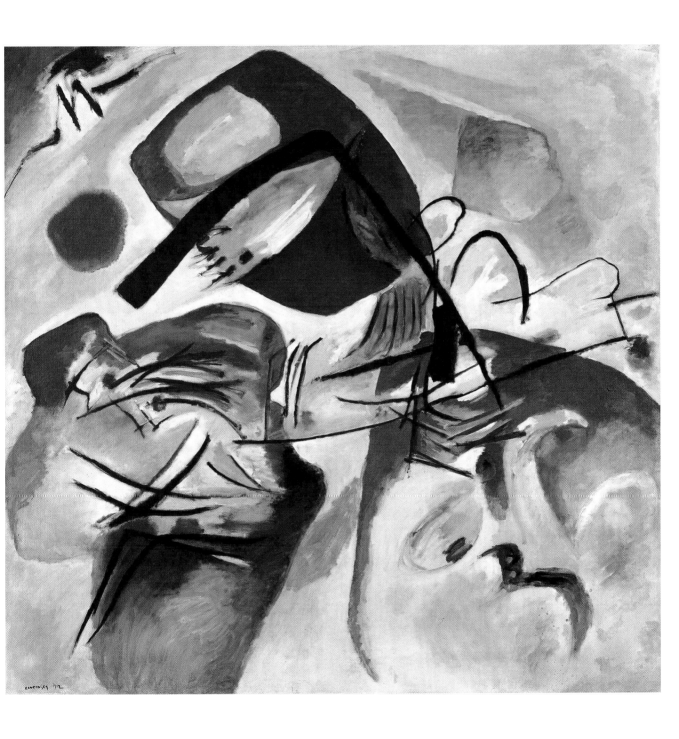

∧
Robert Delaunay
Paris, 1885 – Montpellier, 1941
Formes circulaires, soleil n° 2
(Circular Forms, Sun no. 2)
1912–13

Glue painting on canvas
100 x 68.5 cm
Gift of the Friends of the National Museum
of Modern Art, 1961
AM 3910 P

>
Fernand Léger
Argentan, 1881 –
Gif-sur-Yvette, 1955
Contrastes de formes
(Contrasts of Forms)
1913

Oil on canvas
100 x 81 cm
Gift of M. and Mme André
Lefèvre, 1952
AM 3304 P

The second wave of Expressionism, Der Blaue Reiter (Blue Rider) movement, originated in Munich in 1911, at an exhibition at the Thannhauser gallery organised by Franz Marc and Wassily Kandinsky. Intellectually and artistically, the Blaue Reiter group (whose other members were Alexei von Jawlensky, August Macke, Gabriele Münter and Marianne von Werefkin) bore the stamp of Kandinsky, who had just finished his important essay *Concerning the Spiritual in Art* (published 1912). In this treatise, he developed two main ideas which were shared by the group as a whole: 'inner necessity' as the principle of the personal life of the artist which conditions his work; and the language of line and colour which must provide the pictorial response to this necessity. For Kandinsky, the artist 'can use any form to express himself' and must proceed in such a way that form is the 'exteriorisation of the inner content'. Although in the Blaue Reiter movement we still find some elements of Die Brücke – landscapes, houses, still lifes – the aim is no longer to rage at reality in images of overpowering candour, but on the contrary to escape from the material world into a spiritual realm attained by pure, eternal art. A consequence of this withdrawal from the material into a mystic dimension is that, as the Fauvist, Cubist or Futurist features melt away, the paintings produced by this group are notable for their shimmering colours, warm tones, soft outlines and harmonious compositions. The vividness of the colours, the strongly contrasting volumes they create and the tension between volume and outline were intended to stimulate a sensual synthesis which sets off a vibration in the observer's soul. To achieve this result, the Blaue Reiter artists conducted rigorous, formal research with the aim of establishing a universal pictorial language not limited by time or place.

In the second decade of the century, Kandinsky produced works which came close to pure abstraction (*Improvisation V*) or were entirely abstract (*With the Black Arch*), supposedly expressing nothing but the inner life of the artist freed of material attachments. At the same time, such disparate artists as Robert Delaunay (*Formes circulaires / Circular Forms*), František Kupka (*Ordonnance sur verticales / Order on Verticals*), Fernand Léger (*Contraste de formes / Contrasts of Forms*), Gino Severini

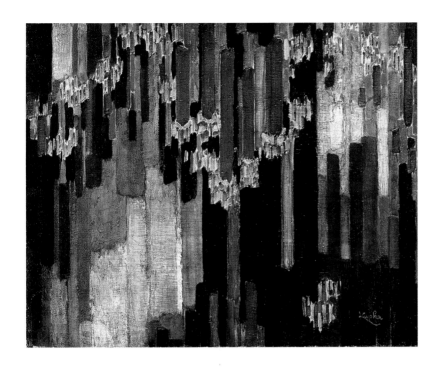

<

František Kupka
Opocno, 1871 – Puteaux, 1957
*Ordonnance sur verticales
(Order on Verticals)*
1911

Oil on canvas
58 x 72 cm
Purchased 1957
AM 3562 P

∨

Gino Severini
Cortona, 1883 – Paris, 1966
*La Danse de l'ours
au Moulin Rouge
(Dancing Bear at the
Moulin Rouge)*
1913

Oil on canvas
100 x 73.5 cm
Purchased by the state, 1950
Attribution 1950
AM 2992 P

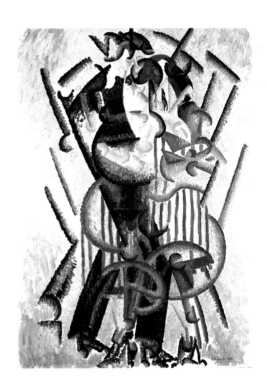

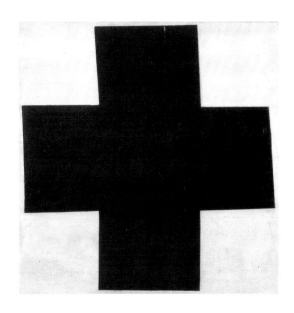

(*Dancing Bear*) and even Francis Picabia (*Udnie*) were experimenting with abstraction, giving free play to the interaction of colours on the canvas without reference to any aspect of exterior reality. Two main non-figurative tendencies, not always easy to distinguish, came to the fore at this time, one giving primacy to gesture, the other based on geometry. Colour was of course not the only issue that led to abstraction, but it was certainly one of the most decisive as artists refused to let it be enslaved to the long tradition of representation.

Kandinsky was the first artist to take this route when he affirmed that the role of art was to tend solely towards the ideal and to abandon materialism in all its forms. Despite their obvious formal differences, many abstract artists shared the desire to break free from reality as perceived by the senses, to transcend it. This is certainly true of Kupka and Mondrian, and also of Malevich (*Black Cross*). These painters were of course exercised by the problems of their medium, but they sometimes went as far as to minimise the material importance of painting, seeing it merely as the means of access to a world beyond appearances. This sort of position was not defended by artists such as Delaunay or Léger, who were interested mainly in the physical constituents of painting and its optical effects. But, generally speaking, the fundamental issue for abstract artists was whether painting was essentially connected with imitation, or whether it could depend on its inherent qualities alone. As a consequence of the non-referential organisation of plastic elements – lines, colours, volumes, blotches, textures – for the first time in the history of Western art artists were not painting with a view to imitation. They were not copying anything found in the real world.

∧
Kasimir Malevich
Kiev, 1878 – Leningrad, 1935
Black Cross
1915

Oil on canvas
80 x 79.5 cm
Gift of the Scaler Foundation and the Beaubourg Foundation, 1980
AM 1980-1

<
Francis Picabia
Paris, 1879 – 1953
Udnie
1913

Oil on canvas
290 x 300 cm
Purchased by the state, 1949
Attribution 1949
AM 2874 P

Matter, Object, Material
1908–1920: from Cubism to Constructivism

A few useful distinctions concerning the use of matters, objects, and materials, together with their concepts.

<

Pablo Picasso
Malaga, 1881 –
Mougins, 1971
*Bouteille de vieux marc
(Bottle of Vieux Marc)*
1913

Charcoal, pieces of paper
pasted and pinned to paper
63 x 49 cm
Gift of Henri Laugier, 1963
AM 2917 D

∧

Georges Braque
Argenteuil-sur-Seine, 1882 –
Paris, 1963
*Nature morte au violon
(Still Life with Violin)*
1911

Oil on canvas
130 x 89 cm
*Gift of Mme Georges Braque,
1963*
AM 4299 P

Although there is no doubt that Picasso's *Demoiselles d'Avignon* (1907, MOMA, New York) was instrumental in the formulation of the new stylistic language that came to be known as 'Cubism' (a term first used in 1911), the trend first came to public attention at an exhibition of works by Braque at the Kahnweiler gallery in Paris in 1908. Writing about Braque's latest canvases of landscapes at L'Estaque, one critic pejoratively noted that the artist 'reduces everything, places and figures and houses, to geometrical schemas, or cubes.' Though unappreciative, he had vaguely grasped what was to become one of the key aspects of Braque and Picasso's joint endeavours between 1907 and 1914: *construction*. Experimenting with geometrical reductions and structures, cut-outs and fragmentation, lines and facets, during this period the two friends redefined the human figure and completely disposed of the laws of perspective, which had dominated pictorial composition since the Renaissance. Their approach was magnificently formulated by Apollinaire in 1913: 'Cubism is the art of painting new compositions with elements borrowed not from the reality of vision, but from the reality of conception'. This concept depended essentially on grasping the different components of the object or person observed (thickness, volume, texture, transparency) – components not evident from a frontal view, which in any case does not exist in reality. By rendering various facets of an object in one and the same painting (Braque, *Nature morte au violon / Still Life with Violin*, 1911 and *Compotier et cartes / Fruit Dish and Cards*, 1913; Picasso,

∧
Georges Braque
Argenteuil-sur-Seine, 1882 –
Paris, 1963
*Compotier et cartes
(Fruit Dish and Cards)*
1913

Oil, pencil and charcoal
on canvas
81 x 60 cm
Gift of Paul Rosenberg, 1947
AM 2071 P

∧ ∧
Pablo Picasso
Malaga, 1881 – Mougins, 1971
*Le Guitariste
(The Guitarist)*
1910

Oil on canvas
100 x 73 cm
*Gift of Jeanne and André Lefèvre,
1952*
AM 3970 P

Le Guitariste / The Guitarist, 1910), the Cubists aimed to give a fragmentary, bit-by-bit vision of it. But, having apparently broken the world down into countless pieces, they recomposed the multiplicity of the visible into a single image. By bringing together both front and rear view, 'folding' planes and making them turn, introducing multiple points of view, exaggerating lines, edges and the graduated transitions between the facets of an object or body, they gave their paintings a *sculptural* quality. This shift from the sculptural to the pictorial, or from the three-dimensional to the flat, was also due to the influence of African sculpture, which is devoid of mimetic intention. In both cases, the aim was not to copy but to conceive a reality different from that which is perceived naturally. In Braque and Picasso's Cubism, the vision is no longer founded on the evidence of sensation alone but derives from a conceptual grasp of reality.

In May 1912, Picasso produced his first 'collage', *Nature morte à la chaise cannée (Still Life with Chair Caning*, Musée Picasso) – featuring a piece of oilcloth printed to resemble chair caning, with a piece of rope for a frame –

and, in September of the same year, Braque completed his first 'papier collé' (paper collage), *Compotier et verre* (*Fruit Dish and Glass*), including three strips of wallpaper imitating wood. For the first time in the history of painting, concrete elements were incorporated into the picture, existing as themselves, giving rise to both optical and tactile sensations. As fragments of external reality, the pasted pieces of paper made the canvas itself a fragment of reality. The painting was no longer a mere image, since it became a piece of tangible reality – what Braque and Picasso called a 'tableau objet' (picture object). Used just as they were, with their colour, texture, density or lightness, the pasted pieces of paper drew the viewer's attention as much to their materiality as to their properties as expressive plastic materials. However, this did not mean that the illusion of reality was totally dissolved, as charcoal lines might be added to the pieces of paper – giving the illusion, for example, that a transparent object was placed in front of them – or they might be used to imitate a completely different material, as in *Bouteille de vieux marc* (*Bottle of Vieux Marc*, 1913), to the canvas of which Picasso pinned a strip of paper in imitation of a fragment of metal frame. The visual, tactile and mental paradox derives from the fact that the pasted pieces of paper, while sometimes giving the illusion of being something else, remain identifiable as the pieces of paper they are. Cubism was profoundly realistic in its use, for both painting and sculpture (e.g. Picasso's sculptures or Laurens's *Bouteille et verre* / *Bottle and Glass*), of relatively easily recognisable materials, such as newsprint, old pieces of wood, plaster, fabric trimmings, wire, sheet metal, cardboard, sand or sawdust mixed with paint (Braque, *L'homme à la guitare* / *Man with Guitar*). It thus paved the way for the object as an autonomous entity and for the use of materials for their own sake.

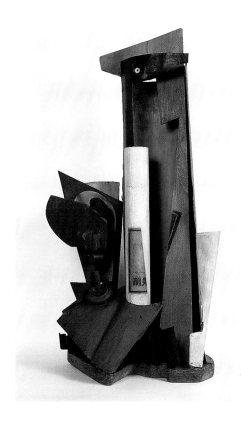

∧
Georges Braque
Argenteuil-sur-Seine,1882 –
Paris, 1963
L'Homme à la guitare
(Man with Guitar)
1914

Oil and sawdust on canvas
130 x 72.5 cm
Purchased with a special state
loan and help from the Scaler
Foundation, 1981
AM 1981-540

>
Henri Laurens
Paris, 1896 – 1954
Bouteille et verre
(Bottle and Glass)
1918

Wood and polychrome
sheet metal
62 x 34 x 21 cm
Gift of Louise and
Michel Leiris, 1984
AM 1984-569

Even though the works they produced in 1912–13 were not widely known at the time, there is no doubt that Braque and Picasso's repeated acts of daring prepared the ground for Marcel Duchamp to elevate an everyday object to the status of work of art. A painter who had formerly been associated with the Cubist and Futurist tendencies, in 1913 Duchamp had the idea – ludicrous in some people's minds, but logical as a continuation of the pioneering gestures of Braque and Picasso – of focusing on the object to the exclusion of any other element which might relate it to painting or sculpture. So he produced *Roue de bicyclette* (*Bicycle Wheel*) – an ordinary wheel with the upturned forks mounted on a kitchen stool – and at about the same time wrote a note asking: 'Can one create works which are not "art"?' This bizarre object was followed in 1914 by *Porte-bouteilles* (*Bottle Rack*), an ordinary bottle rack bought from a department store. These objects were left in Duchamp's Paris studio when he left for the United States in 1915. Once in America, he repeated his gesture, this time exhibiting a snow shovel with the title *In Advance of the Broken Arm*. He referred to it as a 'ready-made', a term he continued to use for other art objects and actions of this kind. As Duchamp himself explained, these everyday objects should not have anything to do with aesthetic pleasure: 'The choice of ready-mades is always based on visual indifference at the same time as a total absence of good or bad taste.' Rejecting any kind of technique, Duchamp also spoke of a 'mental choice' or 'pictorial nominalism', by which he was referring to the possibility of divorcing an object from its context and function, and giving it the status of a work of art purely on the strength of the artist's designation. Although there may have been a large element of provocation and mischievous humour in Duchamp's gesture, it nevertheless raised a whole series of artistic and aesthetic issues which still exercise us today. What is a work of art? What is art? Who decides? When and according to what criteria does an object become a work of art? Although Duchamp did far more than produce ready-mades, his introduction of real objects into the world of art was one of the most cataclysmic acts in 20th-century art.

<
Marcel Duchamp
Blainville, 1887 – New York, 1968
Roue de bicyclette
(Bicycle Wheel)
1913/1964

Ready-made
Metal, painted wood
126.5 x 31.5 x 63.5 cm
Purchased 1986
AM 1986-286

>
Hans Arp
Strasbourg, 1886 – Basle, 1966
Trousse d'un Da
1920–21

Assemblage
Driftwood nailed to wood
and partly painted
38.7 x 274.5 cm
Gift of M. and Mme Christophe
Tzara, 1989
AM 1989-195

<
Marcel Duchamp
Blainville,1887 – New York, 1968
In Advance of the Broken Arm
1915

Wood and galvanised iron
132 x 65 cm
Purchased 1986
AM 1986-289

>
Raoul Hausmann
Vienna, 1886 – Limoges, 1971
Der Geist unserer Zeit –
Mechanischer Kopf
(The Spirit of our Time –
Mechanical Head)
1919

Wooden dummy
and other objects
32.5 x 21 x 20 cm
Purchased 1974
AM 1974-6

The Dada group – the name was picked at random from a dictionary and retained because of its many possible connotations – was founded on 5 February 1916 and originally included the poets Hugo Ball, Tristan Tzara and Richard Huelsenbeck, and the painters and sculptors Marcel Janco, Hans Richter, Christian Schad, Hans Arp and Sophie Taeuber. They were rebelling against art and the established order, and appealing to the irrational. They disseminated their ideas at 'Dada evenings' held at the Cabaret Voltaire, where poets and painters recited poems and staged musical, drama and ballet performances, all deliberately outrageous and calculated to cause scandal. Dadaism spread to many other parts of Europe and the United States, and artists continued to put on events and exhibitions which ridiculed traditional artistic categories, mainly by employing incongruous elements. In their use of materials of little intrinsic value – plaster, embroidery, cardboard, torn-up paper, driftwood (Hans Arp, *Trousse d'un Da*) – the adoption of such

∧
Kurt Schwitters
Hanover, 1887 – Ambleside 1948
*Merzzeichnung 54. Fallende Werte
(Merz Drawing 54. Falling Securities)*
1920

Watercolour, different kinds of paper
and fabric pasted on paper
30 x 22.5 cm
*Purchased 1995
AM 1995-203*

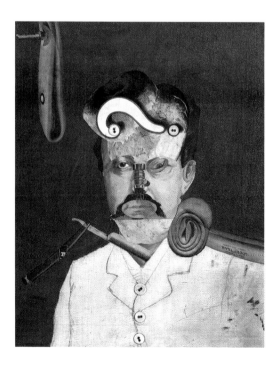

<
George Grosz
Berlin, 1893 –1959
*Remember Uncle August,
the Unhappy Inventor*
1919

Oil, pencil, paper and buttons
glued on canvas
49 x 39.5 cm
*Purchased 1977
AM 1977-562*

ᐯ
Man Ray
Philadelphia, 1890 – Paris, 1976
Lampshade
1919/1954

Painted aluminium
152.5 x 63.5 cm
Given in lieu of inheritance tax 1994
AM 1994-300

>
Sophie Taeuber-Arp
Davos, 1889 – Zurich, 1943
Tête
(Head)
1918–19

Painted wood
34 x 20 x 20 cm
Gift of Marguerite Arp-
Hagenbach, 1967
AM 1692 S

techniques as assemblage (Raoul Hausmann, *L'Esprit de notre temps / The Spirit of Our Time*), collage (Kurt Schwitters, *Merzzeichnung 54 / Merz Drawing 54*) and photomontage (Georg Grosz, *Remember Uncle August, the Unhappy Inventor*), and their subversion of objects and creation of unusual forms (Man Ray, *Lampshade*; Sophie Taeuber-Arp, *Tête / Head*), the Dadaists made an important contribution to broadening the notion of artistic materials. The main characteristic of Dadaist materials was that they were basically junk, retaining traces of their origins even if they were transmuted into collages or assemblages in which they played an expressive role. In works of art, scrap materials, or materials regarded as mediocre or non-artistic (advertisements, posters, photographs, illustrated magazines, children's books, medical encyclopedias, etc.), as in Max Ernst's collages (*La Femme 100 têtes / The 100 Headless Woman*), were deliberately used to blur the aesthetic frontiers between 'great art' and popular culture.

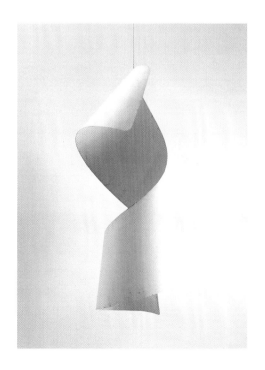

^
Max Ernst
Brühl, 1891 – Paris, 1976
Collage for La Femme
100 têtes (The 100 Headless
Woman), chap. 4,
'Son sourire, le feu, tombera
sous forme de gelée noire
et de rouille blanche sur
les flancs de la montagne'
(Her smile, the fire, will
fall as black frost and
white rust on the slopes
of the mountain)
1929

19.5 x 14.5 cm
Gift of Carlo Perrone, 1999
AM 1999-3 (24)

>
Antoine Pevsner
Oryol, 1886 – Paris, 1962
Construction dans l'espace
(Construction in Space)
1923–25

Bronze and crystal
64 x 84 x 70 cm
Gift of Mme Pevsner, 1962
AM 1346 S

Apart from Duchamp, the work of Cubists and Dadaists hinged on the question of what could and could not be admitted to the rank of artistic material, and why. In this respect, Dada proved bolder in mixing media: everything could be used as matter and material for art. Another, more theoretical, route was taken by the Russian avant-garde, which, emboldened by Cubism and Italian Futurism, played a fundamental role in defining thinking on pictorial and sculptural materials. During the 1910s and 1920s, the Russians actively engaged in practical and theoretical work on materials or, more exactly, on what they preferred to call *faktura* (facture). Concerned with surface workmanship, as well as the texture and reflection, transparency, mass and luminosity of a material, facture was a development of the idea that aesthetic values are not determined by a pre-existing form but are relative to the raw material, the specificity of which conditions the process of constructing the work and the way it is perceived. The material is worked on and exhibited for its own sake, just as it is. For instance, Antoine Pevsner's *Construction dans l'espace* (*Construction in Space*) plays on the ideas of opacity and transparency, lightness and weight, using materials which were new to the sculpture of the period.

The Dissemination of Language
1911–1930: from Cubism to Surrealism

When, in 1911, Braque stencilled some words and letters on a painting entitled *Le Portugais (The Portuguese)*, he was trying to reintroduce a realism that was tending to disappear from Cubism at the time. Cubist works had become so fragmented that the image as a whole was difficult to decipher.

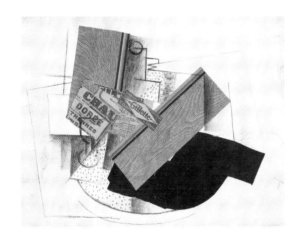

<
Pablo Picasso
Malaga, 1881 – Mougins, 1971
*Tête d'homme au chapeau
(Man Wearing a Hat)*
1912-13

Charcoal, gouache, sand and
papier collé on paper
65 x 49.5 cm
Gift of Henri Laugier, 1963
AM 2916 D

∧
Georges Braque
Argenteuil-sur-Seine, 1882 –
Paris, 1963
*Nature morte sur la table
(Still Life on a Table)*
1914

Charcoal, papier collé on paper
48 x 62 cm
*Given in lieu of inheritance
tax 1984*
AM 1984-354

The idea was quickly taken up by Picasso. Both artists incorporated letters and words, painted or cut from newspapers or magazines, the main function of which was to anchor the viewer's gaze in the picture and provide an element of stability, while allowing them to pursue their research into matters of form, such as the relationship between volumes and flat surfaces. According to Braque, words and letters were perfectly suited to this purpose: 'They were forms in which there was nothing to deform because, being flat components, letters were outside of three-dimensional space and their presence in the picture, by contrast, made it possible to distinguish between objects situated in space from those outside space' (Braque, *Nature morte sur une table, 'Gillette' / Still Life on a Table, 'Gillette'*). This brings us back to the idea that the canvas is above all an 'object' to which the artist applies all sorts of elements alien to traditional painting, but with the difference in this case that the letters, words or, sometimes, a complete newspaper article (Picasso, *Tête d'homme au chapeau / Man Wearing a Hat*) were also *to be read*. For the wording sometimes had an immediate relationship with the canvas as a whole. The fact that words in the Cubism of Braque or Picasso have a decorative or expressive value, a realistic or plastic character, should not obscure their true linguistic aspect. According to its primary definition, a word stands in the place of the thing which it

designates, without of course being the thing itself. A page from a newspaper is of course a 'papier collé', but it is also a text which speaks of entities not visible or palpably present in the picture. But whether painted or pasted on, letters, words and texts were understood by Braque and Picasso to be both raw material and abstract language, sharing the same fate as the other fragmented elements of the canvas, while retaining the meanings inherent in language alone, which were sometimes incomplete, if not totally lost.

The material explosion of language and the dissemination of meaning proposed by the Cubists led the Italian Futurists to what was defined in 1913 by Marinetti as 'parole in libertà', i.e. words set free from any concrete link with punctuation or layout on page or canvas, free of any kind of format, colour or direction. Building on these developments, the Dadaists carried things to a logical extreme and claimed as their own the realm of nonsense. Of course, they maintained the equivalence between plastic and linguistic materials, and this is clearly evident if we compare the collages produced by Hans Arp and Sophie Taeuber-Arp around 1915, in which the positions of the pieces of paper were left entirely to chance, with the recipe for a Dadaist poem issued by Tristan Tzara in 1920: 'To make a Dadaist poem. Take a newspaper. Take a pair of scissors. Select from the newspaper an article of the length you intend your poem to be. Cut out the article. Then carefully cut out each of the words of the article and put them in a bag. Shake gently. Then draw out the clippings, one after another. Conscientiously copy them in the order they emerge from the bag. The poem will be like you.'

The principles of chaos, disorder and the random organisation of materials were applied to works involving language, which seemed to disintegrate, run out of control and lapse into pure nonsense. Just as Dadaist materials respected no hierarchy of values or composition, language too had to take part in these apparently incoherent and meaningless procedures. Photomontage, painting, poetry and sculpture were governed by the only law the Dadaists recognised as being valid: being anti-Dada. If we try to interpret – as one might a word

∧
Raoul Hausmann
Vienna, 1886 –
Limoges, 1971
OFF
1918

Typography on green paper
32.5 x 47.5 cm
Purchased 1974
AM 1974-7

∨
Raoul Hausmann
Vienna, 1886 – Limoges, 1971
ABCD Portrait de l'artiste
ABCD (Portrait of the Artist)
1923–24

Collage
India ink, photographic
reproduction and printed matter
cut out and pasted onto paper
40.4 x 28.2 cm
Purchased 1974
AM 1974-9

∧
Joan Miró
Barcelona, 1893 – Palma
(Majorca), 1983
L'Addition
(The Bill)
1925

Oil on glued canvas
195 x 129.2 cm
Purchased 1982
AM 1983–92

∨
Joan Miró
Barcelona, 1893 – Palma
(Majorca), 1983
La Sieste
(The Siesta)
1925

Oil on canvas
113 x 146 cm
Purchased 1977
AM 1977-203

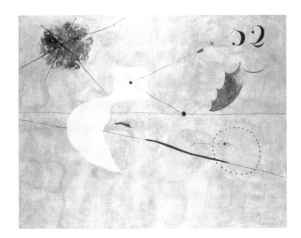

or sentence – Raoul Hausmann's 'poster-poem' *OFF* (1918), the letters seem scrambled and nonsensical, and so do not lend themselves to reading. And yet, their order and the position of each letter seem to suggest that they are intended to be read, from left to right. Are they therefore to be viewed and perceived as an image for their purely plastic value and typographical beauty, or as a text? The small hand symbol pointing to the bottom of the page – a familiar device of printers or advertisers – is placed in sequence with the other letters, although it is really a drawing. But though a pointer, and as such a drawing, it is also an almost verbal sign in a succession of other signs. Although it does not punctuate the sequence of letters in a verbal way, it seems to punctuate the visual space and the organisation of the whole. The photomontage *ABCD*, in which Hausmann's face also features, illustrates another aspect of Dadaist work on language, directly connected with visual perceptions of poster-poems or paintings including language: they are to be read, looked at and *spoken out loud*. This third requirement explains why, in *ABCD*, letters are depicted issuing from Hausmann's mouth. This kind of optical and linguistic experimentation on the part of the Dadaists can be summed up in the celebrated dictum of Tristan Tzara: 'Thought is performed in the mouth.'

Irreverent, and apparently just as absurd, Francis Picabia's attitude to language – adopted before Dadaism, but reflecting Dadaist concerns – was typical of a determination to destroy the sense of reason which sees itself, wrongly according to the adherents of Dada, as sensible and reasonable. When he juxtaposed words and machines, as if the latter were word machines generating text without any purpose or any precise information to convey, he introduced a language divorced from thought. While apparently causing words to function, the machines seem at the same time to scramble and destroy them, making language mechanical. The texts written in *Chapeau de paille* (*Straw Hat*) and *Portrait de Marie Laurencin* are just going through the motions, like the machine. But the machine, like the words that issue from it, though they have no immediate sense or hidden meaning to be deciphered, at least conveys a story. Or rather, it is a cog of history. Producing *senseless* paintings of this kind during or after the debacle of the Great War was not so much a matter of emphasising the loss of all values or creating new ones, but rather affirming the simple fact of existing, of still being. The texts are not defeatist, but on the contrary advocate a life-saving sense of humour and laughter. To the adage 'That which is well conceived comes across clearly', one could reply with Hans Arp's formula: 'Dada wanted to replace the logical non-sense of the men of today with an illogical without-sense'.

Although during his Dada period, beginning in 1912, Max Ernst had become familiar with Freud's writings and produced collages based on associations of ideas and dream formulations, it was not until 1924 that this influence was officially acknowledged by the Surrealists. The fact is that their approach to words in the plastic arts derived essentially from the unconscious procedures analysed by Freud in *The Interpretation of Dreams* (1900). Surrealist works function as in dreams described by the psychoanalyst: either as images, which one then attempts to verbalise, or as words and phrases, from which an increasingly clear overall picture can be derived. So Surrealism sought to give account of a kind of spoken thought, thought expressed in images and by images. The method of the 'cadavre exquis' (exquisite corpse) was the model for this procedure: the technique was to write a few words on a sheet of paper, fold it so that only the end of the sentence was visible, pass it to a neighbour so that he could add his contribution to the text, and so on. This method was also applied to visual 'poems', produced by drawing or by collage. For, in the eyes of most of the Surrealists, there was no difference between poetry and painting, as Joan Miró acknowledged in a series of paintings featuring words or complete sentences, to which he gave the generic name of 'tableaux-poèmes', or poem pictures (*La Sieste*).

But it was undoubtedly René Magritte who, during the 1920s, pushed experimentation with the relationship between words and images to its furthest extreme.

>
René Magritte
Lessines, 1898 –
Brussels, 1967
Querelle des universaux
(The Dispute about Universals)
1928

Oil on canvas
53.5 x 72.5 cm
Purchased 1993
AM 1993-116

Playing on the conventions of language in relation to the things named and perceived, Magritte ran through almost all the possibilities provided by their juxtaposition on the canvas. For him, 'a word can take the place of an object in the real world', 'an image can take the place of a word in a proposition', or 'an object never serves the same function as its name or image'. The title of his humorous *Querelle des universaux* (*Dispute about Universals*) refers to a philosophical debate which began in ancient Greece and reached its height in the Middle Ages. The question was whether the name of a thing applied only to an individual example of that thing or also to things in the plural.

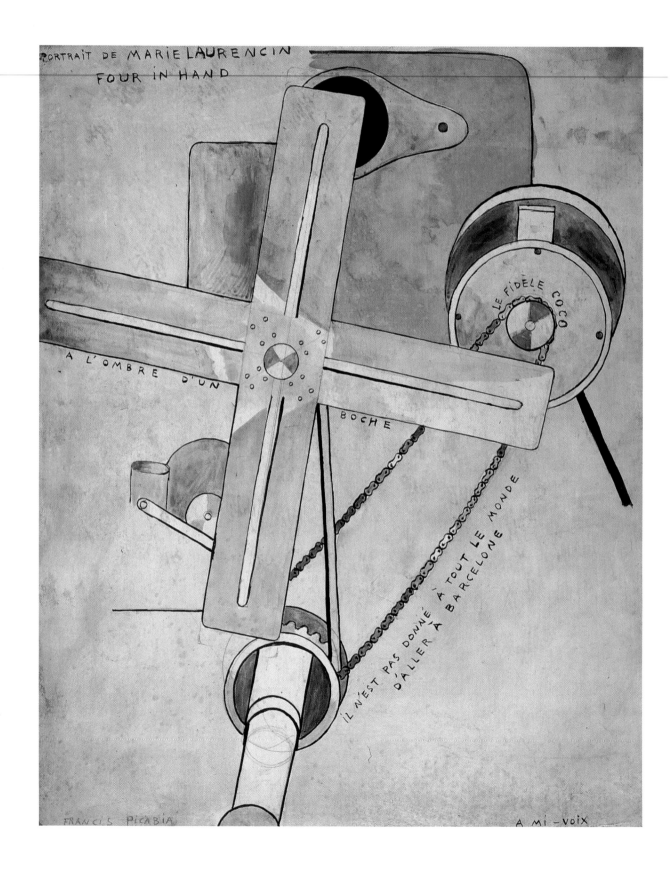

<
Francis Picabia
Paris, 1879 – 1953
Portrait de Marie Laurencin
(Portrait of Marie Laurencin)
1916–17

India ink, pencil, gouache and
watercolour on cardboard
56 x 45.5 cm
Gift of Juan Alvarez de Toledo, 1990
AM 1990-258

∨
Francis Picabia
Paris, 1879 – 1953
Chapeau de paille ?
(Straw Hat?)
c. 1921

Oil and collage on canvas
92.3 x 73.5 cm
Bequest of Dr Robert Le
Masle, 1974
AM 1974-110

∧
Jacques de la Villeglé
Quimper, 1926
Tapis Maillot
(Maillot Carpet)
1959

Torn posters glued to canvas
118 x 490 cm
Purchased 1974
Attribution 1980
AM 1980-428

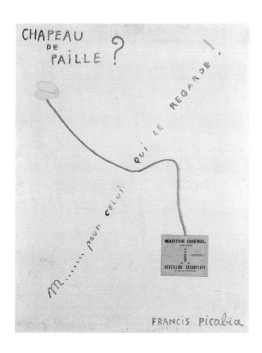

Despite their divergences, these movements had understood that, even if words and letters were deconstructed, cut up, or shown only in part, their meaning could not be eliminated, and that for this very reason the viewer was trapped by the fact of language. Although he might understand nothing of the images perceived, he could not escape (whether or not he was attracted by the picture) from the word or letter, as if the work triggered in him a reflex action obliging him to read. In other words, language was not just another material, for whereas facture belonged in the final analysis to the field of painting, writing was also to be understood as the raw material of language and not just as part of the pictorial field. Finally, the fact that artists had not wanted to draw their vocabulary from professional jargon or erudite terminology, be it literary, sociological or philosophical, demonstrated another aspect of language: its democratisation. This characteristic is to be found later in the torn posters of Jacques de la Villeglé (*Tapis Maillot / Maillot Carpet*). Words do not belong to the language of an élite, but to society as a whole, to us all.

A Utopian View
of People and Objects
1916–1933: from Dada
to the Bauhaus

It is widely held that the fundamental changes in human history have occurred in the fields of science or politics, not in the realm of art.

Nevertheless, the avant-garde movements which emerged during or shortly after the First World War also set out to change the world, despite the terrible setback represented by the war itself. It was no doubt the determination to arrive at what avant-garde artists referred to as the 'new man' that explains the persistence of Utopian projects. These include the Dutch De Stijl (The Style) group founded in 1917, the Bauhaus school, opened in Weimar in 1919, and Russian Constructivism, which began to take shape in 1920. Rooted in the abstract art movement, despite their differences in matters of art theory and ideology, these three streams shared a common interest in achieving a synthesis of the arts and in the idea that their creative work could and should bring about profound changes in society and social relationships. Fortunately, historical events had not destroyed the internal logic of the arts, though it had been strongly affected by them, and although artistic research was again brought to an abrupt halt by the Second World War it was not forgotten by the generation which came to the fore in the 1950s.

To fully understand the aesthetic scope of Dada, De Stijl, the Bauhaus and Constructivism – movements which were linked one to another by exhibitions, periodicals and personal contacts – we must not therefore regard them as simply undertaking theoretical pictorial or sculptural research into colour, line and form, but as pursuing a social and political project. The Dada movement in Zurich and Berlin and the Russian avant-garde of the Bolshevik period brought politics back into 20th-century art with a

^
Georges Vantongerloo
Antwerp, 1886 – Paris, 1965
S x R/3
1933–34

Iron
100 x 100 x 100 cm
Gift of Max Bill, 1980
AM 1980-353

vengeance, and it is fair to describe the artists concerned as socially and politically committed. Merely by deciding to use new materials, refusing to abide by the rules of representational art and preferring abstraction, they were taking up a position vis-à-vis the established order, challenging the way in which works of art were produced and accepted. The outlook of these artists could be described as Utopian because they believed that, by bringing about a radical formal transformation – and here we must include design and architecture – society would also be transformed, leading to a radiant future, or at least a future that was more open and promising.

Although it was not the aim of Dada in either spirit or letter to set up yet another movement or programme, the attempt to rally the various trends or artists of the avant-garde contradicts the charge of nihilism levelled against the Zurich group, though it is

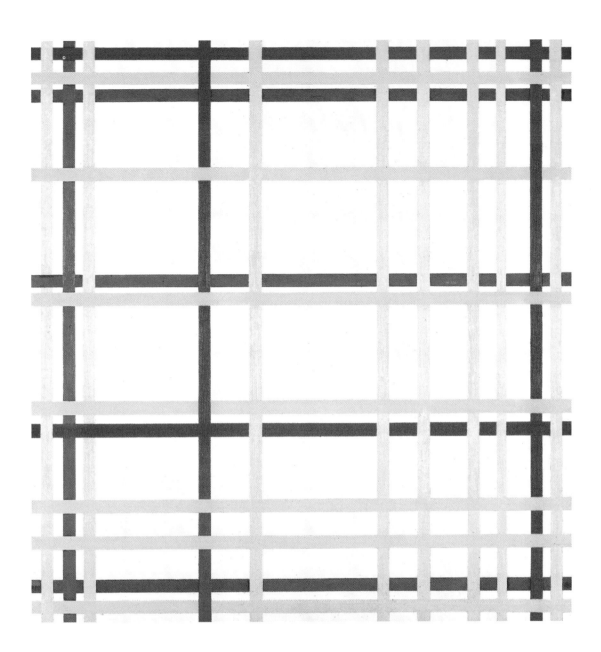

∧
Piet Mondrian
Amersfoort, 1872 –
New York, 1944
New York City
1942

Oil on canvas
119.3 x 114.2 cm
*Purchased with a special loan
and help from the Scaler
Foundation, 1984*
AM 1984-352

true that Dada was long mistrustful of human nature. More voluntarist in outlook – though it was also a question of personalities – the members of the De Stijl, Bauhaus and Constructivist movements were inclined to generalise, if not to universalise, the aesthetic challenge they had taken up. The very name De Stijl implied an entire programme: 'style' was to be applied to painting and sculpture, to be implemented in design as in architecture. Defined mainly by Theo van Doesburg and Piet Mondrian, the programme was to work with simple lines (vertical and horizontal), primary colours (yellow, red, blue) and elementary shapes, surfaces and volumes that could be easily perceived and understood by anyone. Typical examples of this basic style are van Doesburg's *Pure Painting*, Georges Vantongerloo's sculpture *S x R/3*, and one of Mondrian's last paintings, *New York City I*.

>
Paul Klee
Münchenbuchsee, 1879 – Locarno, 1940
Pfeil im Garten (Arrow in the Garden)
1929

Oil and tempera on linen
70 x 50.2 cm
Gift of Louise and Michel Leiris, 1984
AM 1984-557

>
Paul Klee
Münchenbuchsee, 1879 – Locarno, 1940
Rhythmisches (Rhythmus)
1930

Oil on canvas
69.6 x 50.5 cm
Purchased 1984
AM 1984-356

v
Wassily Kandinsky
Moscow, 1866 – Neuilly-sur-Seine, 1944
Gelb-Rot-Blau (Yellow-Red-Blue)
1925

Oil on canvas
128 x 201.5 cm
Gift of Nina Kandinsky, 1976
AM 1976-856

This plastic grammar that could be extended to any artistic production was given the name 'Neo-Plasticism' and its most fervent defender was Mondrian, whose many writings on the subject advocated formal principles dependant on precise content, as it was always necessary to lend form to the experience of reality. In his view, paintings, and art in general, should be conceived on the basis of plastic laws and – over and above geometrical forms – in accordance with a constant equilibrium obtained thanks to oppositional relationships between lines, surfaces and colours, the simultaneous maintenance of continuity and discontinuity, calm and tension, parts and the whole, and a refusal of symmetry. But these plastic laws had psychological and social consequences as, in Mondrian's view, they brought to light the true structure of the world which is hidden from us beneath appearances: 'Balance, by the equivalence of nature and spirit, the individual and the universal, feminine and masculine, the general principal of Neo-Plasticism, is

achievable not only in the realm of art but also in man and society. Where society is concerned, the equivalence of the material and the spiritual can create a harmony hitherto unknown. Neo-Plasticism demonstrates the right order. It demonstrates equity, because the equivalence of plastic means in the composition indicates, for everyone, rights which are of equal value but nevertheless different. Balance through contrary and neutralising opposition annihilates individuals as distinct personalities and so creates the future society as a true unity.'

When, in 1922, Kandinsky became a teacher at the Bauhaus, then situated in Weimar, he entered on a new phase of his career as a painter, geometrising and clarifying the shapes and colours which he had previously worked on more spontaneously and gesturally. But he soon began to mix geometrical elements and free forms, as is evident in *Gelb-Rot-Blau* (*Yellow-Red-Blue*, 1925), a work typical of this period. Also on the staff of the Bauhaus (from 1921) was Paul Klee. During his years as a teacher, Klee had developed a complex system which he incorporated into his paintings and in his more general aesthetic reflections on painting itself. His system of graphic signs with symbolic connotations was based on such elements as lines, arrows, directions and the search for balance and harmony (*Pfeil im Garten / Arrow in the Garden*; *Rhythmisches / Rhythmus*). Not inclined to see painting as potentially leading to a spiritual world beyond the material, László Moholy-Nagy, who also taught at the Bauhaus from 1923 to 1928, was then producing abstract canvases (*Composition A.XX*) in a style akin to that of the De Stijl group and the Constructivists. Using transparent colours, the artist sought to fulfil his longstanding aim to 'paint with light'. Photographer, stage designer, typographer, film-maker and designer, like many artists of the period, Moholy-Nagy played an active part in the social and political movements of the time, directly through his films and in his choice of deliberately modern, avant-garde materials, such as casein plastics, Plexiglas, Bakelite and aluminium, which he used experimentally as a support for paintings and for some of his sculptures.

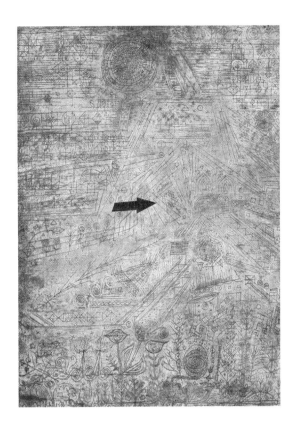

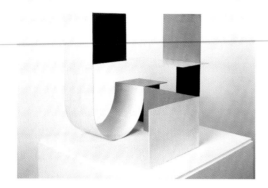

∧

Katarzyna Kobro
Moscow, 1898 –Łódź, 1951
Sculpture spatiale
(Spatial Sculpture)
1928

Painted steel sheeting
44.8 x 44.8 x 46.7 cm
Purchased 1985
AM 1985-18

∧

El Lissitzky
Polchinok, 1890 –
Schodnia, 1941
Study for *Proun RVN 2*
1923

Pencil and gouache on paper
20 x 20 cm
Purchased 1978
AM 1978-28

For an artist, being of one's time therefore meant working with modern materials and forms. This was also an article of belief of the Russian Constructivists, for whom the raw material conditioned a good part, if not all, of the work. Directly influenced by Constructivism (she lived in Russia from 1917 to 1924), in her *Spatial Sculpture* the Polish artist Katarzyna Kobro adopted not only the movement's plastic principles but also its aesthetics. This work is based on a mathematical principle of modular construction using the progression of numbers associated with the medieval mathematician Leonardo Fibonacci (1, 1, 2, 3, 5, 8, 13, etc., obtained by adding the last number to the one before it). Like Moholy-Nagy, El Lissitzky was fascinated by the idea of the artist as engineer and was himself an accomplished architect, designer, photographer and typographer. During the 1920s he developed a series of *Prouns* (the abbreviation of the Russian 'for the affirmation of innovation in art'), such as the study for *Proun RVN 2*, in which he sought to renew the concept of perspective, the nature of the support, and the perception of painting. For Lissitzky, renewing this concept also meant reconsidering one's vision of society, man and what he produces. But it is undoubtedly in Vladimir Tatlin's *Model for a Monument to the Third International* that the Utopian fusion of art and socio-political concerns is most evident. This monument, which was never built, was intended to house the offices of the Komintern. It was to have been a metal and glass construction, four hundred metres in height, consisting of three geometrical structures. Each was designed to turn on itself at a different speed: the cube at the base once a year, the pyramid above it once a month, and the cylinder at the top once a day.

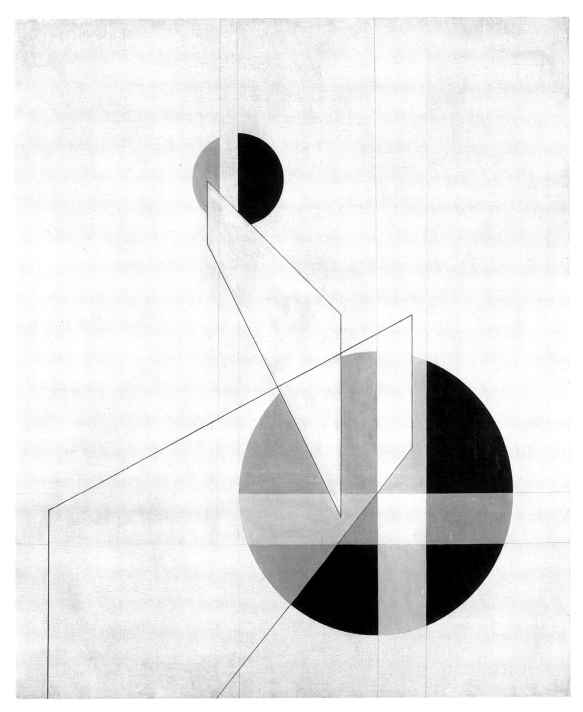

^
László Moholy-Nagy
Borsod (Hungary), 1895 –
Chicago, 1946
Composition A.XX
1924

Oil on canvas
135.5 x 115 cm
*Gift of the Friends of the National
Museum of Modern Art, 1962
AM 4025 P*

Reality and Surreality
1919–1947: from different types of realism to the beginnings of Abstract Expressionism

Given the catastrophic state of Europe in the post-war period, the opposition between the movements discussed earlier was not only formal but also ideological, the war having exacerbated – or perhaps we could say accelerated – the relationship between content and form.

<
Otto Dix
Gera-Untermhaus, 1891 –
Singen, 1969
*Erinnerung an die
Spiegelsäle von Brüssel
(Souvenir of the Galerie
des Glaces, Brussels)*
1920

Oil on canvas
124 x 80.4 cm
*Purchased in memory
of Siegfried Poppe, 1999*
EC-1999-3-AP

Despite their different aesthetic and moral standpoints, the works of the 1920s nevertheless exhibit the common characteristic of being poised between revolt and despair. Lives and dreams had been broken and this resulted in disturbing images of man, bitter criticisms, and an irony and detachment equal to the agony that had provoked them. If we are to understand artistic developments from the end of hostilities to the election of Hitler in 1933, we must continually bear in mind the impact of the Great War on artists' projects, which underwent a profound change of emphasis. Brecht said of the disaster that it had been 'a great practical lesson in the perception of a new vision of things'. This new vision of things and, more generally, this new conception of the world, tended to oscillate between two poles, some elements of which derived from the artistic discoveries of the pre-war period: further progress on the route opened up by abstraction, and a continuation of figurative painting and its themes. Although figurative painting had been overshadowed by the triumph of non-figurative art in the second decade of the century, it nevertheless continued to exist throughout Europe and, after 1919, the figuration that prevailed was one reconsidered in the light of the terrible events of the

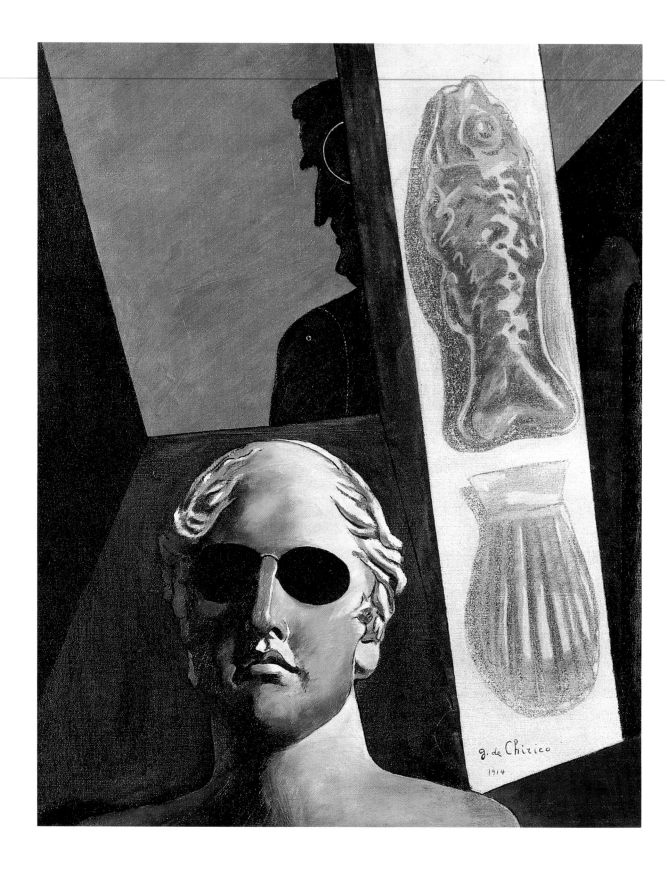

<<
Giorgio de Chirico
Volos (Greece), 1888 – Rome, 1978
*Portrait prémonitoire de
Guillaume Apollinaire
(Premonitory Portrait of
Guillaume Apollinaire)*
1914

Oil on canvas
81.5 x 65 cm
*Purchased 1975
AM 1975-52*

<
Giorgio de Chirico
Volos (Greece), 1888   Rome, 1978
*Ritratto dell'artista con la madre
(Portrait of the Artist with his
Mother)*
1919

Oil on canvas
79.7 x 60.4 cm
*Purchased 1992
AM 1992-58*

<
Pablo Picasso
Malaga, 1881 – Mougins, 1971
*La Liseuse
(Woman Reading)*
1920

Oil on canvas
166 x 102 cm
*Collection of Baron Kojiro Matsukata,
transferred to the National Museum
of Modern Art under the terms of
the peace treaty with Japan, 1959
AM 3613 P*

time. What was generally termed the 'return to order' should rather be referred to as the 'realist movements', to cover both the return to classical painting and many of the avant-garde formal characteristics of the pre-war period, which had not disappeared. Giorgio de Chirico, for instance, was one of the first to return to a form of classicism after his 'metaphysical painting' of the war years, creating works which also had considerable influence on the Surrealists (*Portrait prémonitoire de G. Apollinaire / Premonitory Portrait of G. Apollinaire*; *Ritratto dell'artista con la madre / Portrait of the Artist with his Mother*). Also regarded as one of the artists responsible for a return to the grand tradition in painting, Picasso nevertheless continued to produce canvases mixing the formal discoveries of his Cubist period with neoclassical elements (*La Liseuse / Woman Reading*).

It was above all in Germany that the streams contributing to a profound redefinition of the human image flowed together, beginning with the artists of the first wave of Expressionism, Die Brücke. On the whole, the works they produced individually during the 1920s retained traces of the years they had spent working as a group, though in a less violent mode. The angular lines, garish colours and impasto effects had softened somewhat, and their painting consequently lost much of its force. At the same time, so-called 'independent Expressionist' artists of the same generation, such as Max Beckmann, Otto Dix and Georg Grosz, produced much stronger, more violent and shocking works, taking as their subject matter urban scenes, contemporary social events and the war. In both theme and treatment, there is no doubt that their brothel scenes, rapes, self-portraits, portraits of friends, tortures, murders, crimes of passion and soldiers in the trenches belong not only to Expressionism but also to what was variously described as 'critical realism', 'Naturalism', 'verismo' or Neue Sachlichkeit (New Objectivity).

Whatever their particular brand of realism, all these artists sought, albeit with very different materials, to bear witness to the same human experience: the rage of despair that made them hate war and its catastrophes and led them to denounce man's inhumanity to man in contemporary society. In 1925, Grosz wrote: 'The exponent of verismo holds up a mirror to his contemporary to let him see his ugly mug. I drew and painted from a spirit of contradiction, and through my work I tried to convince the world that it is ugly, sick and deceitful.' The term Neue Sachlichkeit (New Objectivity) – coined by the director of the Mannheim Kunsthalle, Gustav Hartlaub, who organized the first exhibition devoted to the movement in 1925 – evinced a desire to render the truth of the real world in its toughest and most ordinary aspects, distorting them as little as possible and casting an *objective* eye on people, things and events. This explains why a Neue Sachlichkeit painter like Schad (*Graf Saint-Genois d'Anneaucourt / Count Saint-Genois d'Anneaucourt*) developed the practice of photography, the better to capture the phenomena of the real world. The quest for bare,

>
Christian Schad
Miesbach, 1894 –
Stuttgart, 1982
*Graf Saint-Genois d'Anneaucourt
(Count Saint-Genois d'Anneaucourt)*
1927

Oil on wood
86 x 63 cm
*Purchased 1999
EC-1999-3-AP*

unadorned truth is also evident in the work of Otto Dix, who painted cruel pictures of middle-class life (*Erinnerung an die Spiegelsäle von Brüssel / Souvenir of the Galerie des Glaces, Brussels*) and the intellectual élite (*The Journalist Sylvia von Harden*), emphasising the raw facts and pettiness of human existence.

At around the same time, other thinkers were seeking release from the oppression of reality in what they termed 'surrealism' (Apollinaire in the preface to his play *Les Mamelles de Tirésias*, 1917) or 'surreality' (the writer Y. Goll in 1918, referring to Mallarmé) – terms which did not go unnoticed by André Breton, even if the activities of the movement he promoted some years later were rather different. For the thing which completely transformed the 'surrealist' aesthetic into full-blown 'Surrealism' was the modern discovery of the unconscious. To claim that many 20th-century works of art would not have taken the direction they did but for Freud's discoveries of the unconscious and his methods of accessing it is no mere retrospective speculation. And though Surrealism was one of the first movements in art to draw consistently on Freud's discoveries, the first links between the thought of the father of psychoanalysis and some of the future leaders of Surrealism were established before the movement was launched (i.e. before the publication of Breton's *Surrealist Manifesto* in 1924). The process began, as we have already seen, with Max Ernst, and then with André Breton. The latter became indirectly familiar with Freud's ideas (he could not read German) in 1916 when he was working in the psychiatric department of a hospital, and he later used them in his first manifesto. Adopting the format of a dictionary entry, Breton wrote: 'Surrealism, noun. Psychic automatism by which it is intended to express, verbally, in writing, or in any other way, the true functioning of the mind. Thought dictated in the absence of any rational control, and outside of any aesthetic or moral preoccupations. / Philos. Encycl. Surrealism is based on a belief in the superior reality of certain forms of association hitherto neglected, in the omnipotence of dreams, and in the disinterested working of the mind. It tends to ruin permanently all other psychic mechanisms and substitute itself for them in solving the principal problems of life.' As formulated by Freud, the theory of the unconscious

<
Otto Dix
Gera-Untermhaus, 1891 –
Singen, 1969
*La Journaliste Sylvia
von Harden
(The Journalist Sylvia
von Harden)*
1926

Oil and tempera on wood
121 x 89 cm
Purchased 1961
AM 3899 P

<
Victor Brauner
Pietra-Naemtz (Romania),
1903 – Paris, 1966
*Loup-table
(Wolf-Table)*
1939-47

Wood and parts of a stuffed fox
54 x 57 x 28.5 cm
*Gift of Jacqueline
Victor-Brauner, 1974
AM 1974-27*

v
Alberto Giacometti
Stampa (Switzerland) 1901 –
Coire (Switzerland), 1901
*Boule suspendue
(Suspended Ball)*
1930-31

Wood, iron and rope
60.4 x 36.5 x 34 cm
*Purchased 1996
AM 1996-2058*

opened up a deep wound in human reason by explaining that all actions and thoughts were merely the result of urges and deeply buried fantasies. The ultimate reality of man was the unconscious. So the Surrealists sought to bring to light through literature, painting, collage, film, and found or subverted objects (*Loup-table / Wolf-Table* by Victor Brauner) the true psychic life of the human being. The encounter with the ideas of Freud was undoubtedly most evident in the work of Catalan artist Salvador Dalí, who worked to develop a method of painting founded on a delirious interpretation of reality, which he referred to as 'critical paranoia'. Using this technique, he painted his famous 'double images', in which a head can also be a fruit dish, a group of sitting people a face, or a woman's body a horse (*Invisible Lion, Horse, Sleeping Woman*). In the first issue of the periodical *Le Surréalisme au service de la révolution* (July 1930), Dalí published 'L'Âne pourri' (the rotting donkey), a text in which he explained his method, which incidentally influenced a young psychoanalyst who drew on it for his doctoral thesis, published in 1932: Jacques Lacan. As the unconscious had become, one might say, the new raw material of the artist, the Surrealist aesthetic came to be built on processes modelled on the association of ideas, dreams, hypnosis and chance, as well as the personal obsessions of the individual. This led to the production of 'objects with a symbolic function' which transposed sexual fantasies (Giacometti, *Boule suspendue* / *Suspended Ball*), or images which seemed to come directly from the dreams of their creators (Max Ernst, *Chimera*). But it needs to be understood that Surrealist sculptures and paintings did not represent a flight from the reality of this world but, on the contrary, a return to the ultimate reality, that of the unconscious, from which all desire and all existence stem.

The Surrealists therefore sought to express the unconscious directly using all sorts of procedures to bypass reason, as in the automatic drawings of André Masson (1925). Masson, who had drawn inspiration from the 'automatic writing' first practised by Breton and Soupault in 1919 in their joint text *Les Champs magnétiques* (Magnetic Fields), tried to render the movements of mental fantasy in ink drawings in which his hand travelled rapidly over the paper serving as an oscillograph of the unconscious. *Les Chevaux morts* (*The Dead Horses*) is an equivalent in the medium of paint. Automatic techniques obviously emphasised the gestural: Masson in his drawings was no longer depicting a figurative or abstract world on paper but actively presenting gesture. The way the drawing was projected onto the surface became the subject of the work, and two other important factors – subsequently taken up by other artists in the 1940s – were brought into play: spontaneity and speed of execution.

Due to force of events, purely formal research into gesturality did not develop in Europe but in the United States, as a result of the influx of a number of Surrealist painters, in particular Roberto Matta in 1939 and André Masson in 1941. For despite some isolated experiments (in particular by the American painter Mark Tobey), it was undoubtedly the Surrealists who triggered the decisive

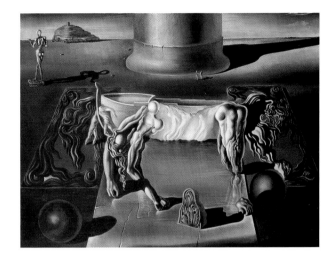

∧
Salvador Dalí
Figueras (Catalonia), 1904 – 1989
*Lion, cheval, dormeuse invisibles
(Invisible Lion, Horse,
Sleeping Woman)*
1930

Oil on canvas
50. 2 x 65. 2 cm
Gift of the Association Bourdon, 1993
AM 1993-26

∨
Max Ernst
Brühl, 1891 – Paris, 1976
*Chimère
(Chimera)*
1928

Oil on canvas
114 x 145.8 cm
Purchased 1983
AM 1983-47

^
Roberto Matta
Santiago (Chile), 1911
Xpace and The Ego
1945

Oil on canvas
202.2 x 457.2 cm
Purchased 1983
AM 1983-94

<
Arshile Gorky
Tiflis (Armenia), 1904 –
Sherman (Texas), 1948
Landscape-Table
1945

Oil on canvas
92 x 121 cm
Purchased 1971
AM 1971-151

<
André Masson
Balagny, 1896 – Paris, 1987
Les Chevaux morts
(The Dead Horses)
1927

Oil and sand on canvas
46 x 55 cm
Gift of Michel and Hélène
Maurice-Bokanovski, 1983
AM 1983-326

interest in automatic drawing and gestural expression. Rothko claimed to have made some automatic drawings in 1938, a year before the arrival in New York of Matta, who then introduced artists such as Motherwell, Pollock and Gorky to automatic writing. One of Gorky's paintings, *Landscape-Table*, is strangely akin to some of Matta's paintings from the late 1930s. Paintings of this kind by Matta, or his *Xpace and the Ego*, which dates from the American period of Surrealism, were to influence many works produced by the American Expressionist painters from the mid-1940s on, particularly as regards line and the movement of the hand over the canvas. In 1939, at a time when many Surrealist events were taking place in New York, Breton wrote a warning article, 'Prestige d'André Masson', in a double issue of the Surrealist periodical *Minotaure*, in which he declared: 'It is high time to react against the idea of the work-of-art-at-so-much-the-yard, which, like a roll of tape, can never run out . . . and replace it with the work-of-art-as-event.' The art scene in America was therefore ready for the advent of the country's first truly modern works: Jackson Pollock's drip paintings.

Body, Figure, Gesture
1925–1965: from Brancusi to Abstract Expressionism

The human body underwent many distortions, deformations and disfigurements at the hands of the avant-garde movements, but these were simply plastic conventions, stages in redefining the notion of 'representation'.

> **Henri Matisse**
Le Cateau-Cambrésis, 1869 – Nice, 1954
Nu de dos, 2e état
(The Back II)
1913

Bronze
188 x 116 x 14 cm
Purchased by the state, 1964
Attribution 1970
AM 1712 S

< **Willem de Kooning**
Rotterdam, 1904 – East Hampton, 1997
The Clam Digger
1972

Bronze
151 x 63 x 54 cm
Purchased 1979
AM 1978-735

For the body to be represented, it must be present in some shape or form in the work of art. It must be possible to recognise its main features, even if they are simplified to an extreme, as in Matisse's *Nu de dos II (The Back II)*, in which he avoids the complexity of a frontal view. This did not of course prevent him from subtly interweaving human and geometrical forms, as in *Figure décorative sur fond ornemental (Decorative Figure against Ornamental Background)*, in which he plays on the terms and on the perceptual relationship

<
Henri Matisse
Le Cateau-Cambrésis, 1869 –
Nice, 1954
*Figure décorative sur fond
ornemental*
*(Decorative Figure against
Ornamental Background)*
1925–26

Oil on canvas
130 x 98 cm
Purchased by the state, 1938
Attribution 1938
AM 2149 P

>
Alberto Giacometti
Stampa (Switzerland), 1901 –
Coire (Switzerland), 1966
Femme debout II
(Standing Woman II)
1959–60

Bronze
275 x 32 x 58 cm
Purchased 1964
Attribution 1970
AM 1707 S

∨
Germaine Richier
Grans (Provence), 1904 –
Montpellier, 1959
L'Orage
(The Storm)
1947–48

Bronze
200 x 80 x 52 cm
Purchased by the state, 1949
Attribution 1949
AM 887 S

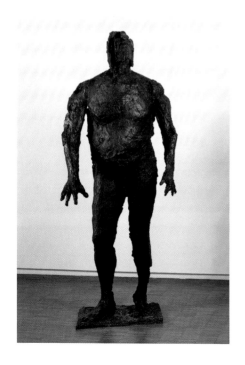

established between figure and background. Sculpture had been essentially abstract since the 1920s and until the late 1940s, with the exception of Matisse, Picasso (*Petite fille sautant à la corde / Girl Skipping*), Henry Moore, Germaine Richier (*L'Orage / The Storm*) and Giacometti (*Femme debout II / Standing Woman II*), there were few major figurative sculptors – or at any rate sculptors who integrated parts or aspects of the human body into their works, as did Lipchitz (*Figure*), Brancusi (*Le Commencement du monde / The Beginning of the World*)

>
Jacques Lipchitz
Druskininkai (Lithuania), 1891 –
Capri, 1973
Figure
1926-30

Painted plaster
220 x 95 x 75 cm
Gift of the Jacques and Yulla
Lipchitz Foundation, 1976
AM 1976-822

∨
Constantin Brancusi
Pestisani-Gorj (Romania), 1876 –
Paris, 1957
Le Commencement du monde
(The Beginning of the World)
1924

Polished bronze
19 x 28.5 x 17.5 cm
Bequest of Constantin Brancusi, 1957
AM 4002-63

<
Julio González
Barcelona, 1876 – Paris, 1942
Femme se coiffant I
(Woman Doing her Hair)
c. 1931

Welded wrought iron
168.5 x 54 x 27 cm
Gift of Roberta González, 1953
AM 951 S

∧
Jean Fautrier
Paris, 1898 – Chatenay-Malabry, 1964
L'Écorché (Corps d'otage)
Écorché (Body of Hostage)
1944

Oil on pasted paper on canvas
80 x 115 cm
Donated in lieu of inheritance tax 1997
AM 1997-93

∨
Jean Dubuffet
Le Havre, 1901 – Paris, 1985
Le Métafisyx
1950

Oil on canvas
116 x 89.5 cm
Purchased 1976
AM 1976-12

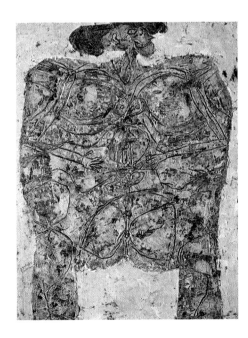

or González (*Femme se coiffant / Woman Doing her Hair*).
The image of the human body was in some cases so
manipulated by the artist, as in de Kooning's *Clam
Digger*, as to be on the boundary between incor-
poration and decomposition, traditional representation
and abstraction of form. We also encounter this
problem of semi-abstract figurability in the paintings of
Fautrier (*L'Écorché*) and those of Dubuffet's 'matiériste'
period (*Le Métafisyx*). The human figure was also

 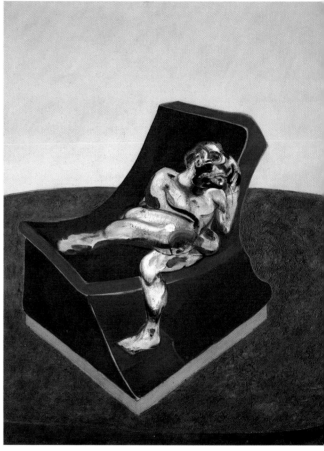

powerfully called into question in the works of Francis Bacon (*Three Figures in a Room*), which combine elements of the human, the animal and the inanimate. An even larger question overshadows this proliferation of works. Rather than an issue of form, the real question – whether they are abstract or figurative, or a mixture of the two – is the more open and ambivalent one of the figure and figuration.

∧
Francis Bacon
Dublin, 1910 – Madrid, 1992
Three Figures in a Room
1964

Oil on canvas
198 x 441 cm
Purchased 1968
Attribution 1976
AM 1976-925

Whereas abstract painting had never entirely divested itself of figuration, abstract sculpture had clearly challenged one of humanity's oldest activities – carving the human figure in stone or wood – which suddenly seemed to be heading for extinction. For it was not only the image of the body and the visual aspect of it that were disappearing, but also its *form*, or in other words a concrete presence which, in art, is the nearest thing to the live human body. No doubt the issues then facing abstract sculpture were much wider-ranging – think, for instance, of ready-mades, the problem of materials and the new techniques to which they were giving rise, and formal issues such as movement (Calder, *Mobile on Two Planes*) – but the paradox is worth emphasising despite the internal logic of art. This leads to another question: does representation imply figuration? Also, the notion of the presence of the body in a work of art had to be reconsidered in terms of the formal discoveries of abstraction. Whereas figuration, as a genre, had in the past implied the presence of the body, and not merely the concreteness of the processes of its representation, abstract art threatened the presence of the body – far more than had been the case with the Fauves or Cubists – because it eliminated the image or form of it from the canvas or sculpture. But if we do not confine ourselves to figuration or the representation of the body in discussing its presence in a work of art, and if we consider in wider terms the idea of projecting the body onto a surface or into a volume, we may then question whether the body had really *disappeared* from 'non-figurative' art. Formats, textures, distances, materials – all these tactile sensations, as opposed to purely optical ones – depend on the bodies of the producer and viewer of the work.

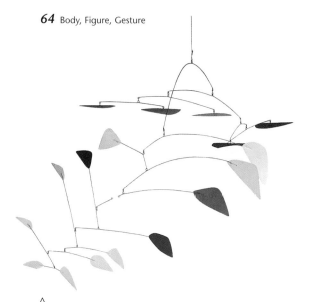

∧
Alexander Calder
Philadelphia, 1898 – New York, 1976
Mobile on Two Planes
c. 1955

Suspended mobile
Painted aluminium sheeting and steel wires
200 x 120 x 110 cm
Gift of the artist, 1966
AM 1514 S

>
Jackson Pollock
Cody (Wyoming), 1912 –
Long Island, 1956
Number 26 A – Black and White
1948

Paint dripped onto canvas
205 x 121.7 cm
Donated in lieu of inheritance tax 1984
AM 1984-312

∨
Hans Hartung
Leipzig, 1904 – Antibes, 1989
T. 1935-1
1935

Oil on canvas
142 x 186 cm
Purchased 1977
AM 1977-2

The conjunction of a concrete space and a non-figurative space also gave greater freedom to hand and arm, freeing gesture from the illusory space implied by figuration. Gesture could then exist in its own right. Going beyond the paintings of Masson, gesture is even more clearly evident in the abstract works first produced by Hans Hartung in 1927 using India ink, and in his oil paintings from the 1930s (*T. 1935 – I*) up to the beginning of the Second World War. There is no denying that Hartung contributed to the liberation of gesture and the rapid application of the pictorial material, half symbol half splash of colour. And the work that emerges is the immanent result of such gesture. A gesture cannot be represented, nor imitated. A gesture is just performed, and what we then perceive on the support is simply its actualisation, the transition to action, the action itself.

Following the Surrealist experiments taken up and developed by the Americans, the challenge was increasingly to free the body – of both producer and viewer – in its relationship with the support. And it was through abstraction that artists sought to achieve a new relationship with the body, by integrating it into the space of the work of art. This meant that an image of the body was no longer necessary in the sense that the body present in front of the work was part of its space. The canvas was no longer an object of contemplation, but gradually became a physical space drawing in the whole body of the viewer, not just his sense of sight. In this respect, Pollock's drip paintings, begun in 1947, were exemplary of what the critic Harold Rosenberg first referred to in 1952 as 'Action Painting', in which the act of painting was seen as more important than the result.

Several of Pollock's interpreters have insisted that his drip-painting methods were not adopted to create an image, however abstract, but that drip painting had no legitimacy except as pure gesture. The essential thing was not the final work but the action or event. Nevertheless there is a perfect coincidence between the procedures and the tangle of signs on the canvas. With this network of lines (*Number 26 A*), Pollock undoubtedly dealt a fatal blow to painting as an art of representation, because what we actually see does not imitate, copy or represent, and has no reality except

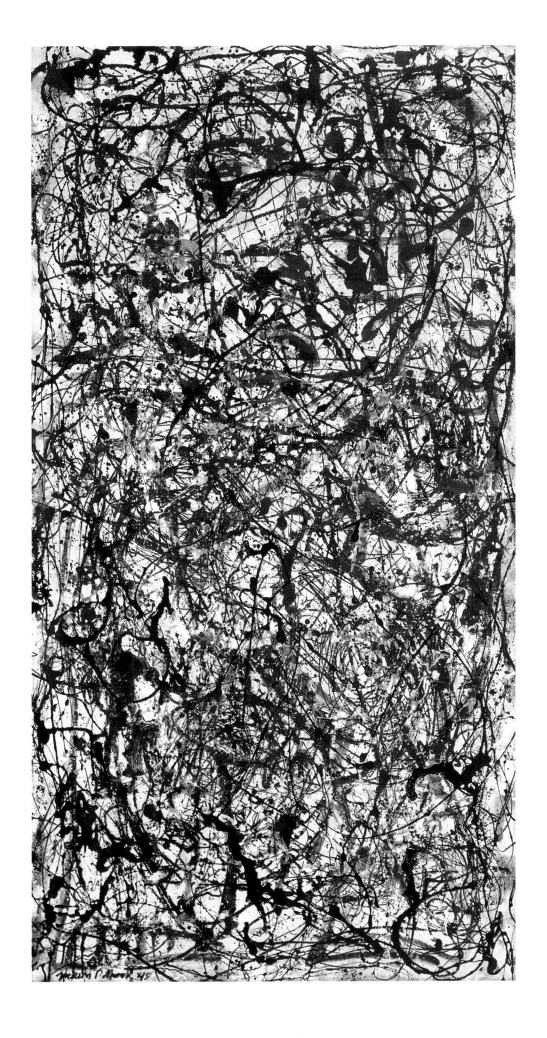

that of the process employed to produce it. What we see is therefore not the image of the process, but the traces – now fixed and frozen – of the process. Applied and interwoven layer by layer, these apparently chaotic features are simply the bodily deployments, movements, positions and postures adopted by Pollock around, in and on the canvas. The spontaneous products of a body in movement, his drip paintings are, from this point of view, strictly *figurative*, not because they are images of a figure but rather the figured traces of a body – and of a body that is alive. When Pollock moved around the canvas, his was not a body turning around another body, but a body within another body, writing all its movements on a virgin surface, in such a way that the canvas had no existence except through the successive and repeated passing of his body over a surface which had literally to be travelled.

In addition to Action Painting, or Abstract Expressionism, which was the most important of the abstract trends which developed in New York in the 1950s and 1960s, two other creative processes emerged: 'Hard Edge' and 'Colour Field Painting'. Despite the differences between these trends, a large number of paintings can be roughly categorised as either 'gestural' or 'geometrical'. These descriptions have not been coined for mere convenience or ease of classification, but because the raw materials – their scale, texture and gestural or geometrical properties – were the result of quite definite and very different aesthetic projects. It is true that the works of Willem de Kooning, Mark Rothko,

>
Barnett Newman
New York, 1905 – 1970
Shining Forth (to George)
1961

Oil on canvas
290 x 442 cm
Gift of the Scaler
Foundation, 1978
AM 1978-371

∨
Ellsworth Kelly
Newburgh (New York), 1923
Eleven Panels, Kite II
1952

Oil on canvas
80 x 280 cm
Purchased 1987
AM 1987-560

Barnett Newman and Ellsworth Kelly are abstract (gestural and/or geometrical), but here again we can also point to the retention of a degree of naturalism. This is evident in Kelly's paintings (*Eleven Panels*), often inspired by photographs of the city or of vegetation, in the constant interplay of the figurative and non-figurative (de Kooning), and in an appeal to the sublime and transcendent (Newman). Therefore, although most American abstract painters were concerned with the 'crisis of subject matter', issues of 'what to paint' and 'how to paint' – which might be either complementary or mutually exclusive – the social and moral values attributed to their works could not always be summed up as 'existential' questions, as then understood, i.e. in the Sartrian sense of the word (his works were available in translation in the 1950s). If we consider two artists of the same generation, the question of existence is treated very differently by de Kooning, who was conversant with current Sartrian ideas, and Newman, who believed in a transcendence beyond human understanding.

\>
Pierre Soulages
Rodez, 1919
Peinture, 195 x 130 cm,
9 octobre 1957
(Painting, 195 x 130 cm,
9 October 1957)
1957

Oil on canvas
195 x 130 cm
Gift of the artist to
the state, 1957
Attribution 1957
AM 3568 P

∨
Georges Mathieu
Boulogne-sur-Mer, 1921
Les Capétiens partout
(Capetians Everywhere)
1954

Oil on canvas
295 x 600 cm
Gift of the Lacarde gallery, 1956
AM 3447 P

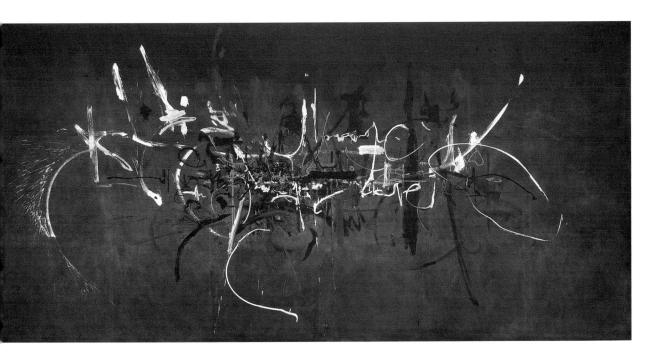

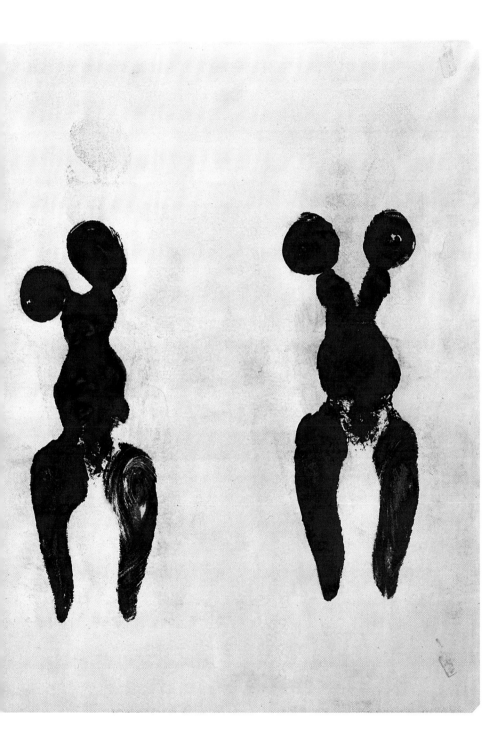

^

Yves Klein
Nice, 1928 – Paris, 1962
Anthropométrie de l'époque bleue (Ant 82)
(Anthropometry of the Blue Period [Ant 82])
1960

Pure pigment and synthetic
resin on pasted paper on canvas
156.5 x 282.5 cm
Purchased 1984
AM 1984-279

^
Yves Klein
Nice, 1928 – Paris, 1962
Ci-gît l'espace
(Here Lies Space)
1960

Painted sponge, artificial flowers
and gold leaf on panel
125 x 100 x 10 cm
Gift of Mme Rotraut Klein-
Moquay to the state, 1974
Attribution 1975
AM 1975-5

In their very different ways, Pollock (*Number 26 A*),
Newman (*Shining Forth*) and Rothko (*Dark Over Brown no.*
14) sought to incorporate the viewer, in particular by
using scale and an almost uniform colour field. Though
absent as an image, the body is present in this
redefinition of the boundaries between perceived object
and perceiving subject. Whereas any painting or
sculpture involves a greater or lesser projection of the
artist's body into a raw material, seeking this projection
by means of gesture on canvas reinforces the
incorporation of the artist, as can be seen in the work of
Georges Mathieu (*Les Capétiens partout / Capetians*
Everywhere), Pierre Soulages (*Peinture / Painting*) or

>
Piero Manzoni
Soncino, Cremona, 1933 –
Milan, 1963
Achrome
1959

Kaolin on pleated canvas
140 x 120.5 cm
Purchased 1981
AM 1981-36

∨
Lucio Fontana
Rosario de Santa Fe
(Argentina), 1899 –
Varese (Italy) 1968
La Fine di Dio
(The End of God)
1963–64

Oil on canvas
178 x 123 cm
Donated in lieu of
inheritance tax 1997
AM 1997-94

Antoni Tàpies (*Large Brown Triangle*). The term 'incor-poration' is perfectly appropriate, to the extent that an artist can integrate, merge or introduce himself into the canvas or sculpture by leaving his mark upon it (Yves Klein, *Anthropométrie* and *Ci-gît l'espace / Here Lies Space*), or without faithfully inscribing upon it the form which was at the origin of this action. For instance, the slashes made by Lucio Fontana in his canvases or the perforations in his *Fine di Dio* (*Death of God*) series result from the physical action of the artist, who seeks not to destroy the canvas but to open it onto a space beyond. Acting in reverse, in accordance with his personal mythology, Piero Manzoni's *Achromes* appear to have absorbed his body and the space around it.

If abstract painting means representing nothing of the visible appearance of reality, not imitating sense data, not giving a mimetic rendering of what exists in the real world, then gestural painting would come into this category. But to the extent that it bears the marks of a body, could not have been made without the presence of this body and is in a sense the imprint of it, does it not in fact include a physical, figural part of the body in question?

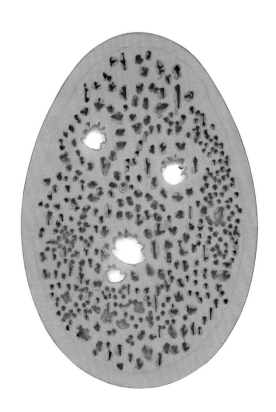

These are the things we are fighting for

Images and Mass Culture
1947–1975: Pop Art, Nouveau Réalisme, Figuration Narrative

During the period when notions of the figure and figuration were being redefined, there emerged a new approach to reality conveyed by the imagery of consumer culture.

The use of everyday, popular images by Braque and Picasso and the Dadaists and Surrealists, as well as the advertisements created by some of the Russian Constructivists (Rodchenko, Lissitzky), had of course prepared the ground, but the concept of 'mass culture', which was born in the United States at the end of the 1930s and then spread slowly and surely until its full triumph in the 1950s, completely transformed their ideological and artistic status. Because of the terrible necessity of events, but also because of the curious logic of his career, it was Kurt Schwitters, the creator of the one-man Merz movement and an artist spiritually akin to Dada, in exile in England since 1940, who first created collages heralding a new vision of an image-consuming society. Schwitters, in addition to using British magazines, cut pictures from the reviews and illustrated papers he received from a friend in the United States. Works such as *En Morn* (a fragmentary title taken from the label of a Golden Morn can of tinned fruit), which already incorporated popular imagery, influenced the British Pop artists. As early as 1947 (one year before Schwitters's death), one of these artists, Eduardo Paolozzi, created collages which included advertisements – in particular for Coca-Cola – fragments of comic strips and cheap novels, company logos, different styles of typography, and all the imagery that was to become the stock-in-trade of Pop Art.

<
Kurt Schwitters
Hanover, 1887 –
Ambleside, 1948
En morn
1947

Collage of different types of paper
32 x 26.5 cm
Purchased 1995
AM 1995-204

^

Jacques Monory
Paris, 1934
Meurtre n° 10/2
(Murder no. 10/2)
1968

Acrylic on canvas
and mirror
160 x 400 cm
Gift of the artist, 1975
AM 1975-96

The term Pop (= Popular) Art was first used in the mid-1950s by the British art critic Lawrence Alloway, not with reference to works of art inspired by popular culture but to the products of consumer culture themselves. However, the term was taken up in 1955 by the Institute of Contemporary Art (ICA) in London and subsequently applied to the works of Richard Hamilton, Eduardo Paolozzi, Peter Blake, David Hockney, Peter Phillips, Allen Jones and Ronald B. Kitaj at two epoch-making art shows: 'This is Tomorrow' (1956) and the 'Young Contemporaries Exhibition' (1961). Though it is true that Pop Art was rooted and propagated mainly in Great Britain and the United States, it had notable repercussions on the early works of, among others, Sigmar Polke and Gerhard Richter in 1960s Germany,

and on the Nouveau Réalisme (New Realism) and
Figuration Narrative movements in France. This latter
tendency, formed in 1965 around the painters Gérard
Fromanger, Jacques Monory, Bernard Rancillac and Hervé
Télémaque, was strongly marked by television, film and
the print media, and was a great deal more politicised in
its choice of subjects (Jacques Monory, *Meurtre n° 10/2 /
Murder no. 10/2*; Bernard Rancillac, *Suite américaine /
American Suite*). Anglo-Saxon and European Pop Art was
on the whole characterised by similar backgrounds
(capitalist societies), similar subject matter (cultural
artefacts, consumer goods, logos, advertising material,
designs, stars), as well as recurring techniques and
processes (silkscreen, photography, enlargements, and
the use and misuse of everyday objects).

∧
Bernard Rancillac
Paris, 1931
*Suite américaine
(American Suite)*
1970

Acrylic on canvas
195 x 402 cm
*Purchased by the state, 1973
Attribution 1976
AM 1976-1005*

>
Jasper Johns
Allendale (South Carolina)
1930
Figure 5
1960

Encaustic paint and newspaper
pasted onto canvas
183 x 137.5 cm
Gift of the Scaler Foundation, 1976
AM 1976-2

It was undoubtedly in the United States that Pop Art found its full expression, but there too it received its initial impetus from the painters of the 1920s, such as Stuart Davis and Gerald Murphy, who had already used advertising material in their cold, precise paintings. But the prime movers were Jasper Johns and Robert Rauschenberg, who in the 1950s began including images of everyday objects in their works (strip cartoons, the national flag, pages from newspapers, throw-away objects, Coca-Cola bottles). Known primarily for his paintings of the American flag, Johns used an encaustic technique to create canvases representing alphabets, figures, targets and maps of the US – elements which were already two-dimensional before being transformed into pictorial images. He also included such everyday objects as chairs, brooms, cups and plates in his compositions. In its size and technique, *Figure 5* is an ironic comment on the gestural emphasis of the Abstract Expressionist painting then in vogue, while at the same time representing a form between abstraction and figuration, between everyday image and formalist image, in which painting for painting's sake (two-dimensionality, colour, composition, process) become the subject of the canvas, and the figure 5 a mere pretext.

Rauschenberg's *Oracle*, made in conjunction with Billy Klüver, needs to be seen as an extension of the invention in 1954 of what the artist called 'combine paintings' – works deriving from both painting and sculpture, or perhaps from stage sets and choreography, incorporating junk materials and personal items, the imagery of consumer society, stuffed animals, and sometimes even sound effects. Seen in this light, *Oracle* is simultaneously scenery, installation, music, everyday reality, sculpture, and a stage on which the viewer can circulate bodily. Adaptable to different settings, each having its own autonomy and characteristics, these strange objects are akin to the elements of a stage set combining different art forms. Made at the height of the Pop period – though Rauschenberg was not a Pop artist – *Oracle* shows the other side of consumer culture: the things it rejects.

Although they drew some inspiration from the British movement, and from Johns and Rauschenberg, Claes Oldenburg, Roy Lichtenstein and Andy Warhol were more forceful in developing their subject matter

^
Robert Rauschenberg
Port Arthur (Texas), 1925
Oracle
1962–65

Galvanised sheet metal,
water and sound effects
236 x 450 x 400 cm
*Gift of Mr and Mrs Pierre
Schlumberger, 1976
AM 1976-591*

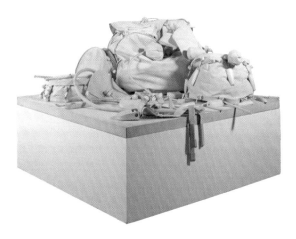

>
Claes Oldenburg
Stockholm, 1929
Ghost Drum Set
1972

Canvas and polystyrene
80 x 183 x 183 cm
Gift of the Menil Foundation in
memory of Jean de Menil, 1975
AM 1975-64

v
Claes Oldenburg
Stockholm, 1929
Giant Ice Bag
1969–70

Vinyl and various materials
600 x 600 cm
Purchased with help from the Scaler
Westbury Foundation, 1999
AM 1999-7

and a popular iconography. Their imagery consisted of everyday consumer items: ice-cream cones, fizzy drinks, sausages, hamburgers, toothpaste, tinned foods, cigarettes, matchboxes, interiors, comic strips and pictures of film stars – all of which provided an instant design, and were part of a market and cultural heritage which everybody could or should be able to relate to. Pop Art played with stereotypes of all kinds and emphasised the ambiguity of art products, in that they displayed a certain anonymity but at the same time possessed the uniqueness we normally associate with works of art.

Although most American Pop artists were ironical about consumer goods, during the 1960s Oldenburg based his work on items of refuse and introduced a connotation of poverty, sometimes introducing the sordid aspects of life, the poverty of his materials gradually extending to the value of the objects themselves. For without sacrificing their humour, his kitsch, pathetic, crazy, ridiculous objects, while leaving little room for the exaltation of merchandise and creature comforts, possessed a sort of cut-price realism. In 1961 he created *The Store*, a space which he used as a workshop and a place for performances or displaying sculpture, where the works were also on sale. Made from fragments of everyday objects and plaster or papier mâché, these works had the appearance of sculptures of pictures or pictures of pictures. In their softness and *behaviour*, many of Oldenburg's sculptures, like *Giant Ice Bag* and *Ghost Drum Set*, are reminiscent of the human body in its capacity for flexibility, movement and change.

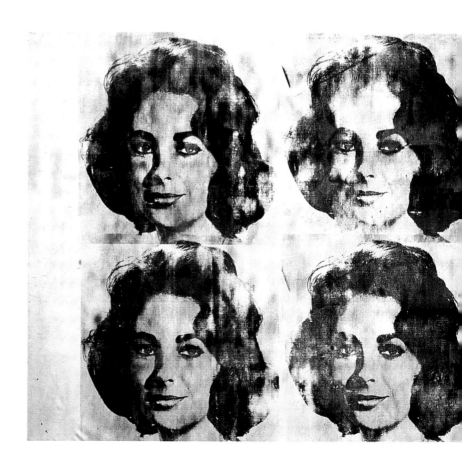

<
Roy Lichtenstein
New York, 1923
*Modular Painting
with Four Panels*
1969

Oil and magna on canvas
274 x 274 cm
Purchased 1977
AM 1977-566

∨
Andy Warhol
Pittsburgh, 1928 –
New York, 1987
Ten Lizes
1963

Oil and lacquer screen-printed
onto canvas
201 x 564.5 cm
Purchased 1986
AM 1986-82

Despite their crafted appearance and disproportionate size, these objects in fact reflected contemporary American society, whose cultural artefacts were first and foremost an image of something rather than the thing itself. They were a ghostly image of the real world, as Oldenburg explained: 'The ultimate act of making things soft is the kiss of death to their functionalism and classicism. The soul of the object, one might say, ascends to heaven in ghostly guise. Its exorcised spirit returns to the realm of geometry.'

In both painting and sculpture, Pop artists aimed to achieve a real transformation of the imagery they borrowed from comic strips and art history (Roy Lichtenstein, *Modular Painting*), advertising and the cinema, the display shelves of department stores and the front pages of daily newspapers. But whatever its original quality, this imagery was always filtered by consumer society, resulting in the artists taking an ambiguous stand. We do not always know if an object is being

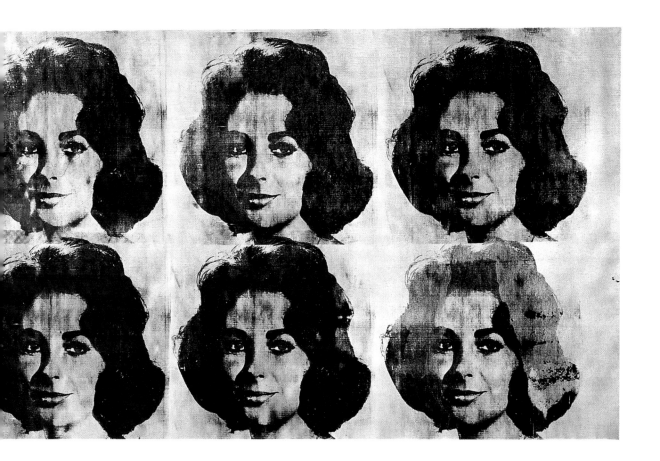

∧
George Segal
New York, 1924
Movie House
1966-67

Plaster, wood, Plexiglas,
light bulbs
259 x 376 x 370 cm
Purchased by the state, 1969
Attribution 1976
AM 1976-1018

appreciated or criticised, if a political or social situation is being glorified or denigrated, as most of their works combine an aestheticisation of reality with a questioning of the factors supposed to make life better and more beautiful. So, for instance, Andy Warhol gives the same pictorial treatment to a portrait of Liz Taylor (*Ten Lizes*) and to the *Electric Chair*. The starting point in each case is a newspaper picture, which the artist elevates to the status of Warholian image – no longer a face or a sinister object but an image hallmarked Warhol. This ambiguous position – between an aestheticised world and the world of pure banality, between the joy of consuming and the fear of being left with nothing – as well as the boredom and violence so typical of the disillusioned outlook of modern society, led some critics to refer to Pop Art as a form of 'capitalist realism'.

Also borrowing from the imagery of mass culture, the works of Edward Kienholz and George Segal, who are

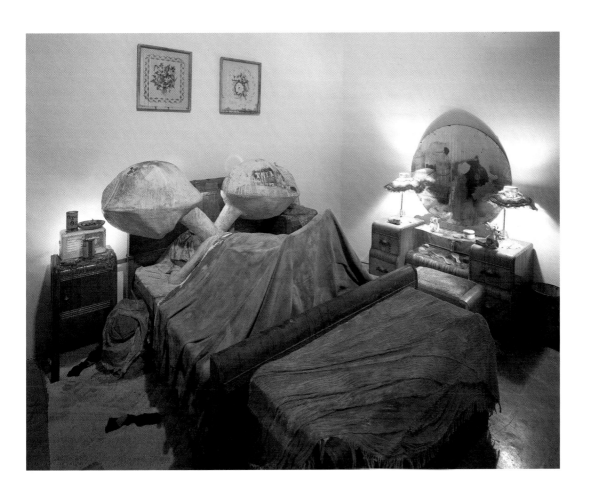

often associated with Pop Art, are striking in their 'disturbing strangeness'. Called 'tableaux' by Kienholz and 'tableaux vivants' by Segal, the common feature of their highly contrasting works is that they are generally made using plaster moulds taken from models and they include real objects from daily life. Frozen in their movements, fixed for ever in their daily gestures (Segal, *The Movie House*), despite the obvious distance established by their being sculpted in plaster, their characters are nevertheless close to us in appearance, almost human. Even though they seem to have stepped out of a nightmare, as in Kienholz's *While Visions of Sugar Plums Danced in their Heads* (a reference to an American Christmas story), their figures are akin to statuary in their form and composition, and in each case the artist tries to retranscribe the concrete, social and psychological factors of their environment, which is thereby transformed into a sort of life-size still life.

∧
Edward Kienholz
Fairfield, 1927 –
Sandpoint (Idaho), 1994
While Visions of Sugar Plums Danced in their Heads
1964

Various materials
180 x 360 x 270 cm
Purchased 1971
Attribution 1976
AM 1976-984

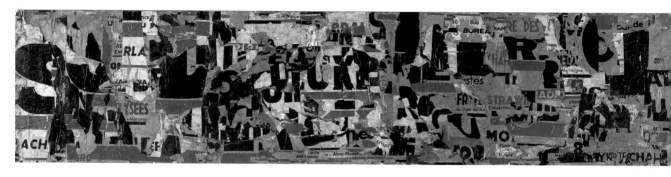

∧
Raymond Hains
Saint-Brieuc, 1926
Jacques de la Villeglé
Quimper, 1926
Ach Alma Manetro
1949

Torn posters pasted to glued
paper on canvas
58 x 256 cm
Purchased 1987
AM 1987-938

∨
Daniel Spoerri
Galati (Romania), 1930
*Marché aux puces:
hommage à Giacometti
(Flea Market: Homage
to Giacometti)*
1961

Chipboard, fabric, various materials
172 x 222 x 130 cm
Purchased 1976
AM 1976-261

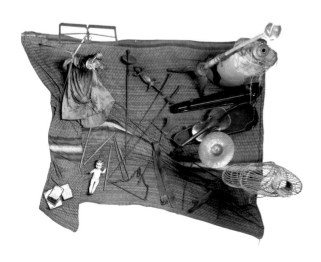

Nouveau Réalisme was born on 27 October 1960, as a result of a founding 'declaration' only a few lines long: 'The new realists have become aware of their collective singularity. New Realism = new perceptional approaches to the real world.' This statement was signed by the artists Arman, François Dufrêne, Raymond Hains, Yves Klein, Martial Raysse, Daniel Spoerri, Jean Tinguely and Jacques de la Villeglé, together with the critic Pierre Restany, who became the group's spokesman. They were soon joined by César, Christo, Gérard Deschamps, Mimmo Rotella and Niki de Saint-Phalle. The Nouveaux Réalistes had begun producing in the mid-1950s and, for the most part, had already arrived at the individual styles and materials we associate with them – factors which, though very personal, ensured their kinship with the other artists in the group. Naturally, the individual approaches of these artists varied widely, but the imagery of consumer culture was the unifying factor and the formula 'new perceptional approaches to the real world' was an accurate summary of their procedures. It was in fact the *realism* of the objects they presented that distinguished their work from British and American Pop Art, and indeed from Figuration Narrative. Their works contained fewer images and reproductions, and more real objects. The torn posters taken from the streets by Hains and Villeglé (*Ach Alma Manetro*) could serve as an emblem of the

Λ
Martial Raysse
Golfe-Juan, 1936
*Soudain l'été dernier
(Suddenly Last Summer)*
1963

Acrylic on canvas, photograph,
straw hat and face flannel
100 x 225 cm
*Purchased by the state, 1968
Attribution 1976
AM 1976-1010*

V
Arman
Nice, 1928
Home, Sweet Home
1960

Gas masks in box covered
with Plexiglas
160 x 140.5 x 20.3 cm
*Purchased with the help of
the Scaler Foundation, 1986
AM 1986-52*

V
César
Marseille, 1921 – Paris, 1998
Ricard
1962

Compression
Crushed automobile (process
directed by the artist)
153 x 73 x 65 cm
*Gift of Pierre Restany, 1968
AM 1968 S*

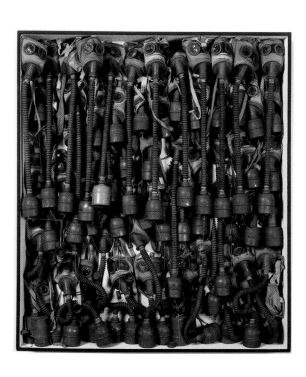

<
Jean Tinguely
Fribourg, 1925 – Berne, 1991
L'enfer, un petit début
(Hell, a Small Beginning)
1984

Various materials
370 x 920 x 700 cm
Purchased 1990
AM 1990-27

general attitude of the Nouveaux Réalistes, who used present reality and the daily environment in all its social, political, resistant, ugly or pleasant aspects, albeit recomposed, transformed or misappropriated. Their styles were not deliberately repetitive, but were attempts to operate systematically in the real world, to draw a social, economic, plastic and political map of reality using the consumer goods and products of modern society. Whether the subject matter was gas masks (Arman, *Home Sweet Home*), cars (César, *Ricard*), leisure time (Raysse, *Soudain l'été dernier / Suddenly Last Summer*), antiques and junk (Spoerri, *Le Marché aux puces / The Flea Market*), or machines so sophisticated that it was impossible to imagine their purpose (Tinguely, *L'Enfer, un petit début / Hell, a Little Beginning*), they present us with a catalogue of our lives as consumers. What we produce is what we are.

Formal Experiments and (Re)definitions of Art
1950–1975: hybrid genres

In many respects, the artistic practices of the 1950s harked back to the spirit of the avant-garde movements of the early part of the 20th century, or to certain specific works, such as the impressive collages of Matisse's final period (*La Tristesse du roi* / *Sorrows of the King*), which continued to influence many artists.

Two major trends began to emerge: one concerned with exploring the specific characteristics of the medium, to the point of calling it into question; the other mixing different media and practices. This rough categorisation applies mainly to the period from the 1950s to the 1970s, which can be described as predominantly 'formalist', in the sense that it was a time of rethinking certain questions and formulating new ones. These included the issues of frame and pedestal

<

Daniel Buren
Boulogne-sur-Seine, 1938
*Cabane éclatée n° 6 :
les damiers
(Exploded Cabin no. 6:
checkerboards)*
1985

Striped material and
wooden structure
283 x 424.5 x 283 cm
Purchased from the artist, 1990
AM 1990-87

>

Henri Matisse
Le Cateau-Cambrésis, 1869 –
Nice, 1954
*La Tristesse du roi
(Sorrows of the King)*
1952

Pieces of paper cut out and
painted in gouache, pasted
onto canvas
292 x 386 cm
Purchased by the state, 1954
Attribution 1954
AM 3279 P

(Kelly, Stella), of painting as a subject for painting (Johns), of the distinction or lack of it between sculpture and painting (Minimal Art, Rauschenberg), of where and how a work of art should be displayed (Buren), of the linguistic character of art (Conceptual Art), and of everyday objects and their elevation to the status of works of art (Warhol). This concentration on form should not be understood as a new incarnation of 'art for art's sake', but as the logical conclusion of the problems raised by the avant-garde movements, as if such formal questions regarding the component parts of a work of art must necessarily be asked. Nor did these artistic developments prevent direct political engagement, against the war in Vietnam for example (Arte Povera, Conceptual Art, Art & Language), or political involvement of an indirect but equally relevant kind, as when the Minimalist artist Donald Judd claimed that his choice of material (corrosion-resistant steel rather than

v
François Morellet
Cholet, 1926
Du jaune au violet
(Yellow to Violet)
1956

Oil on canvas
110.3 x 215.8 cm
Purchased 1982
AM 1982-15

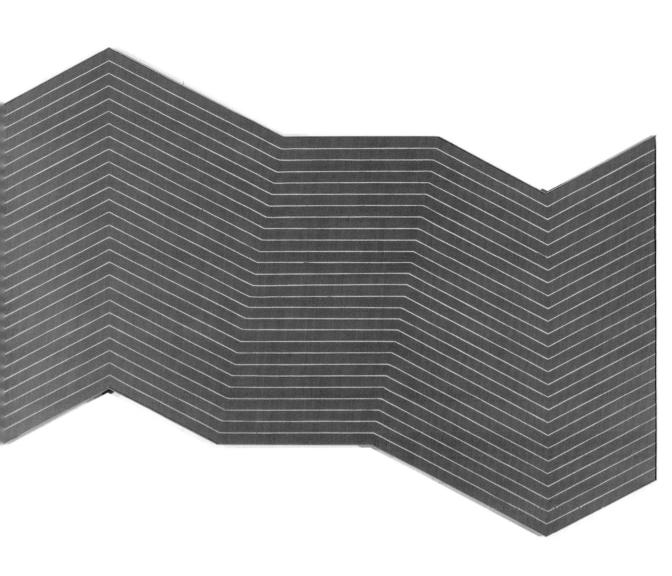

∧
Frank Stella
Malden, 1936
Mas o menos
(More or Less)
1964

Metallic powder and
acrylic on canvas
300 x 418 cm
Purchased with help from
the Scaler Foundation, 1983
AM 1983-95

marble) had political and social implications. Similarly, the human figure continued to be a powerful theme, leading to rewarding developments in both painting and sculpture, as evidenced by the works of Jean Dubuffet, Willem de Kooning and Georg Baselitz. But the once well-established boundaries between figuration and abstraction became blurred, as artists embarked on a complete rethink of their duality or complementarity. In the final analysis, even though some questions were entirely limited to a particular medium – and painting and sculpture returned in force in the 1970s – the themes and genres associated with abstraction, figuration and the object were gradually and deliberately merged as the result of a lack of differentiation between techniques and processes. Hybridisation was the order of the day.

∧
Donald Judd
Excelsior Spring (Missouri), 1928 –
New York, 1994
Untitled
1965

Tinted Plexiglas, 4 steel wire-strainers
51 x 122 x 86.2 cm
Purchased 1987
AM 1987-939

<
Carl Andre
Quincy (Massachusetts), 1935
144 Tin Square

Assemblage: 144 squares of tin laid
out in rows of 12
367 x 367 cm
Purchased 1987
AM 1987-1137

<
Dan Flavin
New York, 1933 – 1996
Untitled (To Donna 5a)
1971

Fluorescent tubes, painted metal
245 x 245 x 139 cm
Gift of Leo Castelli by way of the Georges Pompidou
Art and Culture Foundation, 1977
AM 1977-210

In the space of just a few years, from the mid-1950s to the early 1960s, a new generation of abstract painters undertook a radical re-examination of the components of colour, format, support, technique, and the relationship between the viewer's perception and the work being viewed. The aim might be to reduce the subjective intervention of the artist and the content of the work to a minimum while playing on purely visual effects (Morellet, *Du jaune au violet* / *Yellow to Violet*), or to cut out the stretcher in such a way that the artist had only to reproduce, as if by deduction, the external form conditioning what was inside the painting, which might not correspond – again by an optical illusion – to the cut-out in question (*Mas o menos*, Frank Stella). The rigour of this artist's work, and the problem he first

∧
Robert Morris
Kansas City, 1931
Wall Hanging (Felt Piece)
1969–70

Felt
250 x 372 x 30 cm
Gift of Daniel Cordier, 1989
AM 1989-458

>
Sol LeWitt
Hartford, 1928
5 Part Piece (Open Cubes)
in Form of a Cross
1966–69

Dripped lacquer, painted steel
160 x 450 x 450 cm
Purchased 1976
Attribution 1977
AM 1977-108

raised in 1960 (at the same time as Ellsworth Kelly or Kenneth Noland), as to the redefinition of a cut-out object which is neither painting nor sculpture, paralleled the concerns of the artists who initiated the Minimalist movement in 1965: Carl Andre (*144 Tin Square*), Dan Flavin (*Untitled*), Donald Judd (*Untitled*), Sol LeWitt (*5 Part Piece*) and Robert Morris (*Wall Hanging*).

Despite its name, Minimal Art was not an aesthetic reduced to the forms of objects alone. Although all these artists worked on geometrical figures that could be derived one from another (square, rectangle, triangle, etc.), on developing variations of predetermined structures, on problems of volume, surface and flatness, it would be wrong to jump to the conclusion that these forms reduced to their simplest expression would

necessarily lead to an emphasis on the minimal or the negative. The aim of the Minimalists was, on the one hand, to escape from the age-old categorisation of painting/sculpture and, on the other, to question the very status of art. Without constituting a movement or producing a manifesto, they nevertheless shared a desire to work on a human scale with simple geometrical forms made of contemporary materials which were not illusory,

Brice Marden
Bronxville (N.Y.), 1938
Thira
1979–80

Oil and wax on canvas
244 x 460 cm
*Gift of the Georges Pompidou
Art and Culture Foundation, in
honour of Pontus Hulten, 1983
AM 1983-190*

<<
Richard Artschwager
Washington, 1923
Book III
(Laocoon)
1981

Formica, metal handles,
Leatherette cushion
122 x 71 x 104 cm
Purchased 1984
AM 1984-812

<
Richard Serra
San Francisco, 1939
5 : 30

Corten steel
139 x 230 x 200 cm
Purchased 1983
AM 1983-454

<
Robert Ryman
Nashville (Tennessee), 1930
Untitled
1974

Paint dripped onto canvas
pasted to wood
182 x 546 cm
Purchased 1985
AM 1985-19

or representative objects which were perceived for their own sake and which, in the words of Morris, were real objects in a real space. To the then dominant trend in art, led by Clement Greenberg, who demanded that the specificity of each medium be clearly defined, Donald Judd, acting as the spokesman of the Minimalists, replied in his 1965 treatise *Of Some Specific Objects*: 'Half, or perhaps more, of the best works produced in recent years belong neither to painting nor to sculpture . . . Nowadays, painting and sculpture are no longer so neutral, no longer simple "containers"; they are better defined and are neither incontestable nor inevitable. After all, there are specific, well-defined forms which produce relatively precise effects.' It was therefore in the context of an aesthetic battle for a hybrid art form mixing influences and issues which seemed theoretically impossible (because they were regarded as undesirable by some of the rigorist critics of the time) that other artists – artists very different in outlook from the originators of Minimal Art, such as Richard Artschwager (*Book III*), Richard Serra (*5 : 30*), Robert Ryman (*Untitled*) and Brice Marden (*Thyra*) – were able to flourish and take up and pursue questions old and new relating to 'painting' and 'sculpture'.

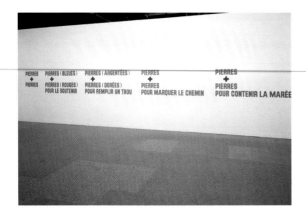

^
^
Lawrence Weiner
New York, 1942
STONES + STONES 2 + 2 = 4
January 1987

AM 1988-959

^
Joseph Kosuth
Toledo (Ohio), 1945
One and Three Chairs
1965

Wood and photographs
200 x 271 x 44 cm
Purchased by the state, 1974
Attribution 1976
AM 1976-987

Also resistant to traditional categories, the Conceptual artists developed a quite different approach, based on the linguistic character of the work of art. The American brand of Conceptual Art, first promoted in 1965 by the publisher Seth Siegelaub, was supported by the artists Robert Barry, Douglas Huebler, Joseph Kosuth and Lawrence Weiner. An English group, Art & Language, founded in 1968, included Terry Atkinson, David Bainbridge, Michael Baldwin and Harold Hurrell. The essential characteristics of Conceptual Art were a refusal to accept art as object-orientated (and the modernist consequences of this concept: materiality, creation of the work by the artist, exhibitions, the critic as expert) and an emphasis on the idea that gave rise to the work. It did not matter whether the work eventually took a physical form or not – for instance *Stones + Stones* by Lawrence Weiner, which could not be realised – whether it remained at the idea stage or left traces of its ephemeral existence in the form of photographs, catalogues, postcards or graph paper. Joseph Kosuth's *One and Three Chairs* is part of a series entitled *Proto-investigations*, in which the artist took an everyday object and placed on either side of it a photograph of the object and its dictionary definition. This way of working was deliberately 'tautological', so that the viewer did not need to use modes of reasoning and perception other than those provided by the actual experience. The viewer understands that the definition may apply as much to the photograph as to the concrete object, or may be a general definition of any chair, i.e. of the idea behind the object. However, the photograph is not the chair (but an image), while the concrete chair corresponds to the definition but is not the whole definition, which is itself an image, as it is an enlarged photograph of the relevant page of the dictionary. There are therefore several possible interactions between images, concrete objects and ideas, and these are the internal components of the work which is submitted to us as a proposal, a definition of itself.

Although the term formalism is not appropriate to the very different works of Daniel Buren, Niele Toroni, Claude Viallat and Claude Rutault, their common concern has been to redefine the constituent parts of their work using a number of basic parameters which were virtually set in stone once the procedures had been

∧
Niele Toroni
Muralto (Switzerland), 1937
*Coups de pinceau
(Brushstrokes)*
1966

Glycerophytalic paint on free-
hanging canvas
198.5 x 195.5 cm
Purchased 1990
AM 1990-324

established. For instance, since 1967 Daniel Buren has been systematically using 'alternating white and coloured stripes each 8.7 cm wide', providing what he calls a 'visual tool' for laying bare what is at issue in a work of art and in artistic intervention. The artist and his work are never neutral or autonomous, as they are always taken from the social and political fabric and submitted to financial, architectural or urban constraints, i.e. to a definite place and context. Therefore, when Buren repaints his stripes, or arranges and applies them in different settings (museums, streets, buildings, trains, walls), his rule is never to repeat the same work, as it is created uniquely for a particular place and that place alone – what he calls a work *in situ*. This rule also applies to his series of *Cabins* (*Cabane éclatée n° 6* / *Exploded Cabin no. 6*), which, even though they can be reconstructed, are never reconstructed in exactly the same way.

In 1967, Niele Toroni developed his particular process, which still consists in applying strokes of a no. 50 brush to a given surface at regular intervals of 30 cm: 'What I call "no. 50 brush mark" is a form which does not exist. I called it that because it is the result of a painting exercise: applying the bristles of the brush, the part used for painting, to the given surface, so that the colour is deposited on it and becomes visible' (*Coups de pinceau / Brushstrokes*). The supports may change (waxed cloth, paper, a wall), but the procedure remains the same, creating a repetition which is in a kind of dialectic tension with the difference. Toroni's work is also concerned with development over time, because, in reiterating his gesture without ever doing the same thing twice, he is recording his own temporality.

∧
Claude Viallat
Nîmes, 1936
Untitled
1966

Impressions on canvas
214 x 257 cm
Purchased 1983
AM 1983-469

∧

Claude Rutault
Trois-Moutiers, 1941
*Toiles à l'unité, 1973/
Légendes, 1985
(Canvases in Unity, 1973 /
Captions, 1985)*
1973-85

6 standard canvases on
stretchers, painted the
same colour as the wall
*Purchased 1988
AM 1988-1063*

In 1966, Claude Viallat began using the form – a sort of bean or palette, *Untitled* – we still find in his recent works. As a result of the neutrality born of his persistence, with this form he has developed a practice which reconsiders the act of painting and the plastic constituents of the canvas – now separated from the stretcher – as well as questions of colour, format, the impregnation of the pigment, and the flexibility of the fabrics he uses, whether tarpaulins, parasols or items of clothing. Repeated on all kinds of textile support, but always different, these strange motifs are used to reveal some of the minimal characteristics of painting.

Rutault's procedure, first adopted in 1973 and still developing, is also a matter of redefining the role of some of the simple but necessary elements of painting: canvas, stretcher and monochrome. To determine the principles of the act of painting, and of the place and context in which he exhibits, Rutault drafted a series of 'definitions/methods', each enunciating a rule. Here for instance is 'definition/method no. 1', dating from 1973: 'A canvas fixed on a stretcher and painted in the same colour as the wall on which it is hung. All the standard formats available in the trade may be used, whether rectangular, round or oval. They are hung in traditional manner.' From this first rule, Rutault formulated others, each new definition/method being both a completely new development and an elaboration of older definitions/methods (*Toiles à l'unité, 1973, Légendes / Canvases in Unity, 1973, Captions*).

In the mid-1960s, a new generation of German painters who were later described as Neo-Expressionists (the group included Georg Baselitz, Jörg Immendorf, Anselm Kieffer, Markus Lüpertz, A.R. Penck and Sigmar Polke) caused something of an upheaval in the artistic landscape, then dominated by American trends (Pop, Minimal, Conceptual). Their technique was deliberately crude and violent, and their choice of subject matter was dominated by the human figure. Not until 1969 did Baselitz begin inverting his canvases, turning people and things upside down as a way of denying content and drawing attention to the purely pictorial aspects of his work. The subjects he chose were very ordinary, without any special qualities or implications.

∧
Georg Baselitz
Deutschbaselitz, 1938
Die Mädchen von Olmo II
(The Olmo II Girls)
1981

Oil on canvas
250 x 249 cm
Purchased 1982
AM 1982-19

>
Gerhard Richter
Dresden, 1932
Chinon no. 645
1987

Oil on canvas
200 x 320 cm
Purchased 1988
AM 1988-593

>
Gerhard Richter
Dresden, 1932
1024 Farben N. 350/3
(1024 Colours No. 350/3)
1973

Lacquer on canvas
254 x 478 cm
Gift of the artist, 1984
AM 1984-285

The fact of painting being in his eyes more important than the motif represented, he set out to forget the motif and make a picture – nothing else. By inverting his pictures, Baselitz was not trying to achieve the effect of an abstract painting, nor even tending towards an abstraction of the motif. The inverted figure was still a figure. What was disturbing was the physical shock conveyed by the artist, who played down any kind of empathy with the figures, reducing them to the status of motifs.

Influenced in the early 1960s by some of the formal aspects of Pop Art, Gerhard Richter soon distanced himself from the movement to work out his own methods, subjects and forms. In 1962 he began using photographic material culled from newspapers, magazines, encyclopedias and family picture albums, or images which he shot himself. He deliberately chose this material for its poor artistic qualities, adapting it to his own ends. Generally projected onto virgin canvas using an episcope, his images were greatly enlarged and pictorially reworked, borrowing from the techniques of photography. His canvases therefore have the fuzziness and movement blur we associate with photography, but are paintings in the full sense of the word (*Chinon*). However, Richter's purpose was not simply to imitate photography but, through his encounter with it, to delve more deeply into painting and to use it, paradoxically, as a photographic medium. Until the mid-1970s, Richter painted in this way or, perhaps we should say, represented images of the main painterly genres: portraits, history paintings, landscapes and still lifes. Since then, in his colour chart (*1024 Colours No. 350/3*) and *Abstract Paintings* series, he has explored the possible *images* of abstract painting – without going about it systematically – to shed a different light on *figurative* works.

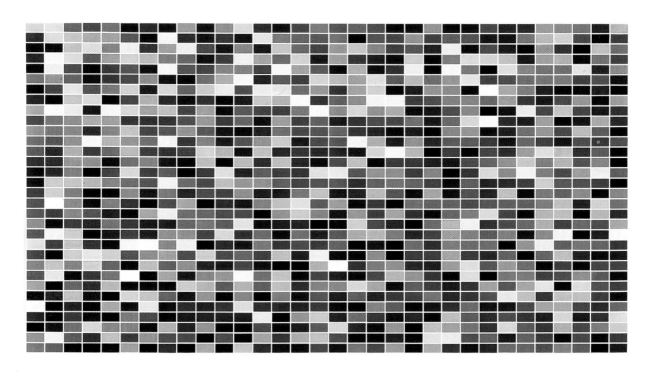

∧
Gérard Garouste
Paris, 1946
Phlegyas, Dante et Virgile
(Phlegyas, Dante
and Virgil)
1986

Oil and varnish on canvas
200 x 235 cm
Purchased 1986
AM 1986-279

Neither nostalgic nor modernist, since the 1980s Gérard Garouste has gone back almost to the origins of painting, including elements excluded and despised by abstract and figurative painting alike: narration and literary interest. A good example is *Phlegyas, Dante and Virgil*, from his *Divine Comedy* series. Though it goes against the modern formalist concept and the tendency to proclaim the death of painting, his attempt is nevertheless another way of redefining the status and ideological and plastic functions of painting, rethinking them in terms that are also formal and destructive, so as to reveal the dead end to which they lead and, paradoxically, the new possibilities they offer.

Arising, in the mid-1960s, from the interaction between painting and photography, the work of Jeff Wall draws heavily on the painting of the mid-19th century, because it was this period that gave rise to our modern pictorial conceptions and to the issues since regarded as fundamental (in particular painting as the subject of painting). Wall took one of these pictorial issues – how to be a contemporary history painter – and gave it a contemporary slant using a different technique. Although his transparency mounted on a light box, *Picture for Women*, is an obvious reference to Manet's *Bar at the Folies-Bergère*, the important thing is not the reference as such but Wall's investigation of the status of pictures, their staging, the place of the viewer in the interplay of perceptions and viewpoints – in fact the relationship between form and content, which was all too often overlooked by an entire stream in modern painting and sculpture. This is partly why Wall chose a medium which was both different and closely bound up with the logic of the visual image.

From the 1950s to the 1970s, the emergence of Performance Art and Action Art confirmed the process of hybridisation that was taking place. From Black Mountain College's *Untitled Event* (1952) to the works of body art produced in the 1970s, the human body was featured in actions (Yves Klein) and 'happenings', for which it served as the raw material. But these activities could also result in environments (Oldenburg), videos (Nauman, Acconci) and installations. This is true of most of the works of Joseph Beuys, which are no longer

v
Jeff Wall
Vancouver, 1946
Picture for Women
1979

Cibachrome transparency,
light box
161.5 x 222.5 x 28.5 cm
Purchased 1987
AM 1987-1135

<
Joseph Beuys
Krefeld, 1921 –
Düsseldorf, 1986
Plight
1985

Installation
43 felt elements, grand piano,
blackboard, thermometer
310 x 890 x 1813 cm
Purchased with the help of
Antony d'Offay and David
Sylvester in memory of
the artist, 1989
AM 1989-545

>
Marcel Broodthaers
Brussels, 1924 –
Cologne, 1976
Salle blanche
(White Room)
1975

Wood, photographs,
paint and light bulb
390 x 336 x 658 cm
Purchased 1989
AM 1989-201

<
Joseph Beuys
Krefeld, 1921 –
Düsseldorf, 1986
Fonds VII/2
1967/1984

Installation
8 piles of felt, metal plates,
wires and copper objects
196 x 455 x 643 cm
Purchased 1985
AM 1985-139

paintings or sculptures in the traditional sense, and in which he sought to embody what he described as 'social sculpture'. By this concept, Beuys was affirming that everybody could be an artist, capable of creativity. He wanted to extend the notion of art to even the most banal activities, embracing ideas and events of a social and political nature. While, through his actions, Beuys's body served as the catalyst for energies that contributed to his personal mythology, art was nevertheless intended to heal the wounds of society and its individual members. His happenings were generally wordless and only afterwards was a dialogue engaged with the audience. *Fonds VII/2*, one of a series of works entitled *Fonds*, is made of materials often used by Beuys because they retained heat and were conductors of energy: 'Stacks of felt are aggregates, and sheets of copper are conductors. The accumulation of heat in the felt functions for me like a generator, a static action. All my *Fonds* serve as a basis or foundation from which other sculptures can be produced.'

Like many artists during this hybrid period, Marcel Broodthaers blended literature, photography, films and environments, drawing inspiration from Dada and Surrealism and from Conceptual Art, to produce works of painting or sculpture while creating environments through which he raised questions about the artistic milieu. *Salle blanche* (*White Room*) is a reconstruction of the artist's home/workshop in Brussels. He described it as 'the most faithful possible reconstitution of a complex made by the artist in 1968 attacking the notions of the museum and of hierarchy.' Broodthaers in fact transformed his apartment, for one year, into an imaginary museum, which nonetheless enabled him to explore the role of the work in a public context and the material and symbolic functions of the artistic setting. The words written on the walls are now the only remaining traces of this ironic action, in which the very structure of an exhibition – the place where works of art are displayed – was called into question.

From the Perishable to the Infinite

1967–1980: Arte Povera, Process Art, installations

Widely adopted by most artists, the mixing of genres shattered the traditional categories of painting and sculpture, and even those who continued to adhere to them had inevitably to take into account the radical transformation that had occurred.

<
Giuseppe Penone
Garessio, 1947
Soffio 6
(Breath 6)
1978

Terracotta
158 x 75 x 79 cm
Purchased 1980
AM 1980-42

∧
Michelangelo Pistoletto
Biella (Italy), 1933
Metro cubo d'infinito
1965–66

Mirror and rope
120 x 120 x 120 cm
Purchased 1990
AM 1990-158

The notions of painting and sculpture were henceforth subsumed into the more open concepts of art and the artistic that led to installations, environments, happenings, processes and attitudes. It was in this context that the Arte Povera (poor art) movement emerged, in 1967. If we accept the official dates for the movement, launched by the Italian critic Germano Celant, it was relatively short-lived – 1967 to 1972 – despite its international impact. As a result of successive exhibitions, the label came to be applied to Giovanni Anselmo, Alighiero Boetti, Pier Paolo Calzolari, Luciano Fabro, Jannis Kounellis, Marisa Merz, Mario Merz, Giulio Paolini, Pino Pascali, Giuseppe Penone, Michelangelo Pistoletto and Gilberto Zorio. The term 'arte povera' was used for the first time in September 1967, by Celant, in the catalogue of an exhibition staged at the La Bertasca gallery in Genoa. Referring directly to the 'théâtre pauvre' pioneered by the Polish director Grotowski, the critic declared that: 'Gesture and mime have been born again, the language of gesture is replacing text; elementary human situations are becoming signs . . . In art, visual and plastic reality is therefore seen as it is; it is reduced to its accessories and is discovering its linguistic artifices.' Reducing things to archetypes, raising the ordinary and

<
Luciano Fabro
Turin, 1936
Piede
(Foot)
1968–72

Murano glass and
shantung (silk)
333.5 x 108 x 79 cm
Purchased 1989
AM 1989-134

>
Mario Merz
Milan, 1925
Igloo di Giap
(Giap Igloo)
1968

Various materials
120 x 200 x 200 cm
Purchased 1982
AM 1982-334

insignificant to the status of art, giving primacy to matter and materials, to the body, to pure presence – these were some of the characteristics of Arte Povera as defined by Celant. Despite the deliberate vagueness of this manifesto, it would be wrong to conclude that 'poverty' implied simply a process of stripping away. In fact, the artists concerned often used aesthetically and intrinsically rich materials, such as mirrors (Pistoletto, *Metro cubo d'infinito*), Murano glass (Fabro, *Piede / Foot*), or marble, bronze, copper and neon lighting (Mario Merz, *Igloo di Giap / Giap Igloo*), and the materials adopted by Arte Povera were certainly no 'poorer' than those used in the collages of Picasso, Ernst, Arp and Schwitters or the 'combine paintings' of Rauschenberg, the environments of Oldenburg and Robert Morris, or the 'accumulations' of Arman. What was different about Arte Povera was the fundamental place it gave to the developmental process of the subject matter and raw materials employed. Whether these were a lettuce (Anselmo, *Untitled*), salt, coffee, plants, animals, stones,

fruits or clay (Penone, *Soffio 6 / Breath 6*), wax, acids or plaster (Paolini, *Caryatid*), coal, wood or wool (Kounellis, *Untitled*), cotton, gas or rubber (Zorio, *Per purificare le parole / To Purify Words*), the emphasis was often on the ephemeral and perishable characteristics of the materials which partly or wholly constituted the work. Autonomy no longer belonged to the work of art alone but to the physical development of each natural element, often not reworked by the artist and presented in the raw state. Where aesthetics were concerned, it was not a question of returning to the state of nature, nor of playing culture off against nature, but of metaphorically – or concretely – including man (we, too, are perishable, transient beings) in the perpetually changeable process of thought. And this aesthetic thinking was concerned with matter, not with manufacturing a physically and conceptually *separate* artefact. Unlike a number of other avant-garde movements in the 1960s and 1970s, Arte Povera did not create 'artefacts', as Minimal Art, Pop Art or Nouveau Réalisme might do, but ductile, soft, malleable materials which could receive for a limited time span the no less ephemeral marks of the hand or body of the person shaping them. The role of the raw material was to retain and display the real imprint of its manufacture or transformation. This was the best way of presenting the 'poverty' of an age-old human gesture: that of transforming the world simply to ensure survival.

∧

Giovanni Anselmo
Borgofranco d'Ivrea, 1934
Untitled (granite, lettuce, copper wire)
1968

Granite, fresh lettuce, copper
70 x 23 x 37 cm
Purchased 1985
AM 1985-177

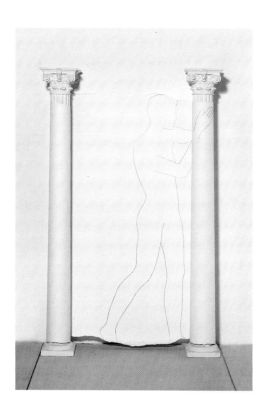

<

Giulio Paolini
Genoa, 1940
Caryatide
1980

Plaster, drawing on Canson paper
182 x 204.8 x 25.5 cm
Purchased 1981
AM 9181-29

A leading representative of Land Art – a tendency which emerged in the early 1970s and was dominated by British and American practitioners – Richard Long works in a natural setting, using materials found *in situ* during the many journeys he has made around the world. He assembles and arranges them in forms generally far removed from those occurring naturally, even though they are sometimes reminiscent of such natural forms. Most of these man-made arrangements are ephemeral, as the resulting works are left where they are, subject to the tender mercies of climate and weather. Photographs are the only surviving witness to Long's work. However, he does sometimes arrange

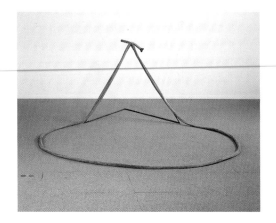

materials in galleries or museums, as in the case of *Cornwall Slate Circle*, consisting of 290 pieces of dressed slate placed in a more or less regular manner on a circle previously drawn on the ground. Constructions created in a natural setting therefore broaden the notion of raw material and of sculpture as a genre, tending to result in fleeting monuments born of the encounter between nature and culture.

Tony Cragg's work could be regarded as that of an archaeologist of modern society, since the materials he uses are essentially junk. Taking account of their colour, weight, density and form, the artist uses these discarded objects as he might use a pigment or charcoal to draw totally new forms. In *Opening Spiral*, the materials are

<
Gilberto Zorio
Andorno Micca, 1944
*Per purificare le parole
(To Purify Words)*
1969

Various materials
170 cm
Purchased 1983
AM 1983-379

>
Tony Cragg
Liverpool, 1949
Opening Spiral
1982

Waste materials: plastic,
wood, metal, fabric
152 x 260 x 366 cm
Purchased 1988
AM 1988-1061

<
Richard Long
Bristol, 1945
Cornwall Slate Circle
1981

Dressed Cornwall slate
Diam. 400 cm
Purchased 1982
AM 1982-130

spread out on the ground, their interaction creating effects of colour and texture in such a way that by their components alone they condition the physical characteristics of the form of the object and refocus attention on their raw materiality.

In the 1970s, Barry Flanagan, another artist concerned with a renewed approach to materials, produced some fragile, fluid works which borrowed from the classic vocabulary of statuary but perverted the concept of the statue as a solid, durable object set on a pedestal to symbolise something of noble import. *Casb 1'67*, for instance (the title refers to the materials used: a canvas bag filled with sand), suggests a column, a standing portrait, or an enlarged object, but its basic properties are opposed to those of modern sculpture: soft, heavy, sagging, destructible.

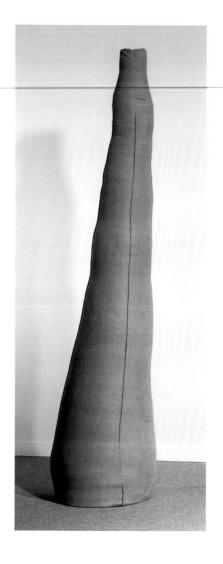

Can a work like Eva Hesse's *Seven Poles* still be described as a sculpture? It is certainly typical of the artist's formal and thematic preoccupations. These generally revolve around references to the body and to certain organic parts, which effectively prolong the tradition of human figuration. During the 1960s, she worked with materials little used by other artists (latex, polyester resin and fibreglass), concentrating on the physical effects of materials, which was unusual at the time. In this case, metal wire armatures have been wrapped in polyethylene, then covered with fibreglass soaked in resin. Though maintaining their abstract characteristics, the translucent appearance, shapes and strong physical presence of these anthropomorphic elements inevitably suggest intestines.

^

Barry Flanagan
Prestatin (Wales), 1941
Casb 1'67
1967

Canvas and sand
260 x 60 x 60 cm
Purchased 1980
AM 1980-5266

^

Eva Hesse
Hamburg, 1936 –
New York, 1970
Seven Poles
1970

Aluminium wires,
polyethylene,
fibreglass, resin
272 x 240 cm
Purchased 1986
AM 1986-248

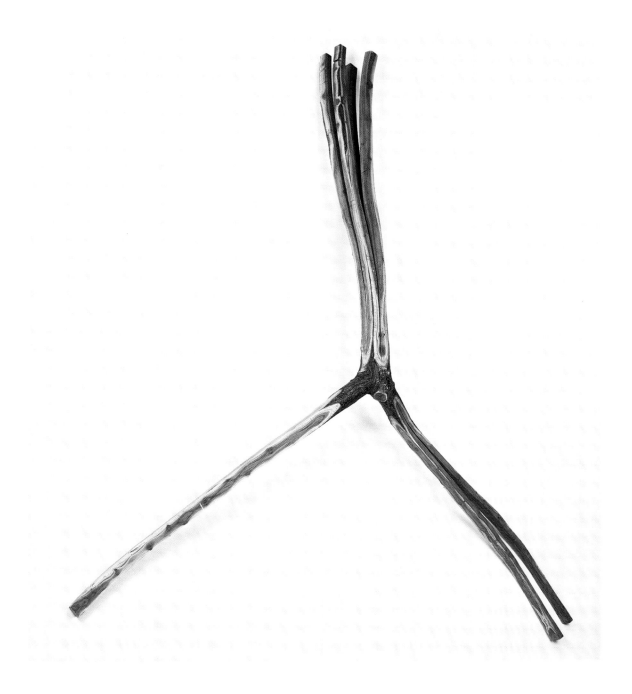

∧
Toni Grand
Gallargues-le-Montueux
(Gard), 1935
*Vert, équarri, équarri
plus une refente partielle,
équarri plus deux refentes
partielles
(Green, squared off,
squared off plus a partial
resplit, squared off plus
two partial resplits)*
1973

Tree branch
164 x 170 cm
Purchased 1983
AM 1983-368

Also concerned with the nature of materials, the work of Toni Grand in the 1970s was based on what he called a 'deconstructive reading' of sculpture. He was then using mainly wood, a material somewhat neglected by most modern and contemporary sculptors. This choice of material was also influenced by his desire to show the manufacturing process, or genesis, of the work, which is contained in its title. *Vert, équarri, équarri plus une refente partielle, équarri plus deux refentes partielles (Green, squared off, squared off plus a partial resplit, squared off plus two partial resplits)* is an account of the different operations performed by the artist on the wood, which could still evolve naturally, without human intervention. This is very much in keeping with Grand's aim, which is to allow the qualities and properties of the material to manifest themselves.

> **Vito Acconci**
New York, 1940
Convertible Clam Shelter
1990

Various materials, lighting
and sound effects
150 x 240 x 280 cm each shell
*Gift of the Friends of the National
Museum of Modern Art, 1994*
AM 1994-262

As well as works created in a natural context and partly or entirely perishable works set up in a museum or gallery, we ought to mention works which cross into the architectural field, thereby giving a further dimension to the notions of painting and sculpture. The common feature of works as different as Vito Acconci's *Convertible Clam Shelter*, Bruce Nauman's *Dream Passage with Four Corridors*, Jean-Pierre Raynaud's *Container zéro* and Imi Knoebel's *Schattenraum IV* (*Shadow Room IV*) is that they all explore spatial and physical notions which are not sculptural in origin, or at least which the notion of sculpture is no longer adequate to explain, even in material terms. Ephemeral or stable,

<

Bruce Nauman
Fort Wayne (Indiana), 1941
Dream Passage
with Four Corridors
1984

Panels, fluorescent tubes,
tables, chairs
283 x 1241 x 1241 cm
Purchased 1987
AM 1987-1136

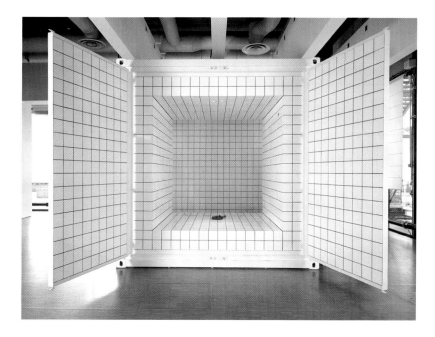

>

Jean-Pierre Raynaud
Courbevoie, 1939
Container Zéro
1988

Tiles and various materials
330 x 330 X 330 cm
Purchased with the help of
the Centre National des Arts
Plastiques, 1988
AM 1988-2(1)

>

Imi Knoebel
Dessau, 1940
Schattenraum 4
(Shadow Room 4)
1988

Hardboard, acrylic on wood
290 x 360 x 300 cm
Purchased 1990
AM 1990-363

composed of natural materials or manufactured, combining artefacts with actions or forming environments,
constructions in dialogue with architecture – the fact that
the works of these artists (and many others) are difficult
to classify into the traditional genres of painting or sculpture is because either they no longer belong there, or
because the genres themselves are in need of a complete
redefinition. Undoubtedly, we sense that some works have

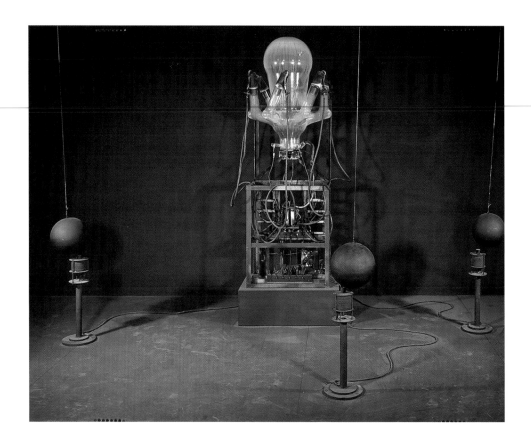

Takis
Athens, 1925
Méduse
(Medusa)
1980

Electromagnetic unit with
mercury-vapour lamp
220 x 60 x 40 cm
Gift of Alexandre Iolas, 1980
AM 1980-547

>
Bertrand Lavier
Châtillon-sur-Seine, 1949
Mademoiselle Gauducheau
1981

Metal cupboards painted with
acrylic paint
195 x 91.5 x 50 cm
Gift of the Friends of the National
Museum of Modern Art, 1987
AM 1987-634

<
Jean Le Gac
Tamaris (Gard), 1936
Story Art (with
Beaux-Arts ghost)
1986

Charcoal, pastel and casein on
paper, film projector and stand
Drawing: 250 x 340 cm
Gift of Daniel Cordier, 1989
AM 1989-426

a formal kinship with sculpture, like Takis's *Medusa*, or with furniture and painting, like Bertrand Lavier's *Mademoiselle Gauducheau,* an artefact painted entirely in acrylic. Or, like Jean Le Gac's *Story Art*, executed partly in charcoal and pastel, they may be based on the narrative tradition of painting. In such cases, the form, the position in space or the isolation of the object, the material, the technique or the way of presenting it invite us to hazard a sculptural or pictorial interpretation. But at the same time, the normal sculptural criteria are too restricted. They are often no longer an issue, since the work will for a time have consisted in distinguishing itself from or effecting a rapprochement with the aesthetic of sculpture or painting. Christian Boltanski's *Les Archives de Christian Boltanski, 1965–1988* (*The Christian Boltanski Archives, 1965–1988*), for instance, or Annette Messager's *Piques* (*Spades*) use non-sculptural or pictorial materials, and the way they are displayed is very different from traditional ways of hanging paintings. So we see that the logic of mixing the arts first introduced by the avant-garde

∧
Annette Messager
Berck-sur-Mer, 1943
Les Piques
(Spades)
1992–93

Various materials
250 x 800 x 425 cm
Purchased 1994
AM 1994-85

>
Christian Boltanski
Paris, 1944
Les Archives de C. B.,
1965-1988
(The C. B. Archives,
1965-1988)
1989

Metal, photographs, printed
matter, lights, electrical wiring
270 x 693 x 35.5 cm
Purchased 1989
AM 1989-551

movements of the early part of the century has led to situations which at first glance seem very strange in pictorial or sculptural terms, but which are really quite simple. Where hybrid works are concerned, either they are just one more metamorphosis of painting and sculpture, or the categories no longer correspond to the artefacts they are supposed to cover, or again these artefacts are mixtures of the two plastic and historic moments. Let it be stressed that neither the absence (presumed or real) of clear criteria and conditions for defining 20th-century painting or sculpture, nor the existence (presumed or real) of works of contemporary painting or sculpture, is preventing the emergence of new formal discoveries and works rich in meaning.

Back to the Future, Again and Again
The last decades

Since the 1980s, it is not so much new techniques (video, computer generated images) or the perfecting of existing ones (photography, moving pictures) that have transformed the artistic landscape as the attitude of artists to their chosen media.

<
Sylvie Blocher
Morshwiller-le-Bas, 1953
*Déçue, la mariée se rhabilla
(Disappointed, the Bride Put
her Clothes Back on)*
1991

Plywood, electric battery, iron,
tulle, neon lighting
Purchased 1996
AM 1996-324

v
Absalon
Devohot (Israel), 1964 – Paris, 1993
*Proposition d'habitation
(Proposal for a Dwelling)*
1992

Plywood, cardboard and acrylic paint
180 x 270 x 370 cm
Purchased 1994
AM 1994-253

The latter have lost their sacrosanct materiality and most artists are no longer obsessed with their technical characteristics. This new attitude can also be ascribed, as we have seen, to the proliferation of artistic hybrids. The possible combinations are so numerous that such terms as mixed media, assemblage, installation, intervention, work *in situ* and multimedia no longer suffice to cover the material and aesthetic range of the works being produced. Factors that make them even more difficult to classify are the proliferation of unusual exhibition venues (swimming pools, hotels, churches, restaurants), and the fact that institutions themselves (museums and art centres) are sometimes the work of art, or the exhibition itself is the subject of the exhibition. Many projects are no doubt more obviously connected with recent issues, such as the question of architecture, areas for the body to move around in and the exhibition venue (Absalon, *Proposition d'habitation / Proposal for a Dwelling*; Michel Verjux, *Petite et grande porte / Small and Large Door*), or challenges to the act of painting involving copying or quotation, a renewal of perception, or a questioning of the status of the image or picture (John Armleder, *Untitled*; Eric Fischl, *Strange Place to Park no. 2*; Bernard Frize, *Sans titre [squelette] / Untitled [skeleton]*). Some artists have taken an archaeological interest in the notion of the pedestal and the artefact itself (Didier Vermeiren, *Untitled*), or have reconsidered the human body in a sculptural transposition of movement (Marie-Ange Guilleminot,

∧
Michel Verjux
Chalon-sur-Saône, 1956
Petite et grande porte
(Small and Large Door)
1984

2 slide projectors, 2 rectangular
wooden structures painted white
Variable dimensions
Gift of the Friends of the National
Museum of Modern Art, 1992
AM 1992-374

∧∧
John Armleder
Geneva, 1948
Untitled
1987

Installation
Oil on canvas and divan
Canvas: 100 x 100 cm
Divan: 69 x 163 cm
Purchased 1988
AM 1988-1062

>
Eric Fischl
New York, 1948
Strange Place to Park no. 2
1992

Oil on canvas
219 x 249.5 cm
Loan from the Fonds National d'Art
Contemporain, 1994
AM 1994-dép. 151

La Rotateuse / Rotating Woman). Even Marcel Duchamp is still remembered in the half-admiring, half-critical work of Sylvie Blocher, *Déçue, la mariée se rhabilla* (*Disappointed, the Bride Put her Clothes Back on*) – a reference to Duchamp's *La mariée mise à nu par ses célibataires, même* (*The Bride Stripped Bare by her Bachelors, Even*) and proof of the link which still exists between some contemporary artists and the historical avant-garde movements.

∧
Bernard Frize
Saint-Mandé, 1954
Sans titre (squelette)
Untitled (Skeleton)
1990

Acrylic and resin on canvas
65 x 54 cm
Purchased 1990
AM 1990-242

Of course, even if fewer are being produced internationally, significant works of painting and sculpture, in the traditionally accepted sense of the term, are still appearing, refusing to allow themselves to be left behind formally and aesthetically by the multimedia genres. Moreover, it is a striking fact that most of them take their place, intentionally or from contextual necessity, in the tradition of historical developments we associate with painting and sculpture. However, the explosion in the production of virtual and synthetic images, and the creation and circulation on the Web of cultural information and artworks on an unprecedented scale, constitute a conceptual and material revolution – and this is not an overstatement – as to what may be regarded as a 'work of art' and, even more so, a work of 'sculpture' or 'painting'. If our rapid review of the last century shows, in the final analysis, that the regular questioning of the notions of painting and sculpture have considerably extended their range, one might justifiably expect that this cycle would be repeated as a result of the introduction of new technologies. Thus multimedia works would, in the first instance, be set against traditional materials (or older technologies), and would gradually be integrated into a period of art history, which would in turn be reconsidered and transformed in the light of fresh technological and artistic inputs. However, there is a danger here (one which has tempted a number of art historians and critics) of seeing these 'repetitions' – identifiable given adequate time and detachment – as marking some sort of 'progression' in artistic matters. This idea is fiercely defended nowadays as it gains strength from the inescapable advance of technical progress, enthusiastically adopted in art, which is unlikely to go away. At this point, two major artistic tendencies seem to be emerging. On the one hand, there are those for whom the 'material', be it highly sophisticated or a straightforward piece of iron or a pigment, continues to condition the work, to some extent at least, but without the work being reduced to it; on the other, there are those who think that only continual new technological discoveries provide suitable material for contemporary art or the art of tomorrow. The first of these two attitudes implies a 'cumulative' effect in the history of art, that is to say it is not possible to return to certain subjects or materials

^
Didier Vermeiren
Brussels, 1951
Untitled
1987

Plaster, steel, casters
165 x 81 x 89 cm
Gift of the Friends of the National Museum of Modern Art, 1992
AM 1992-375

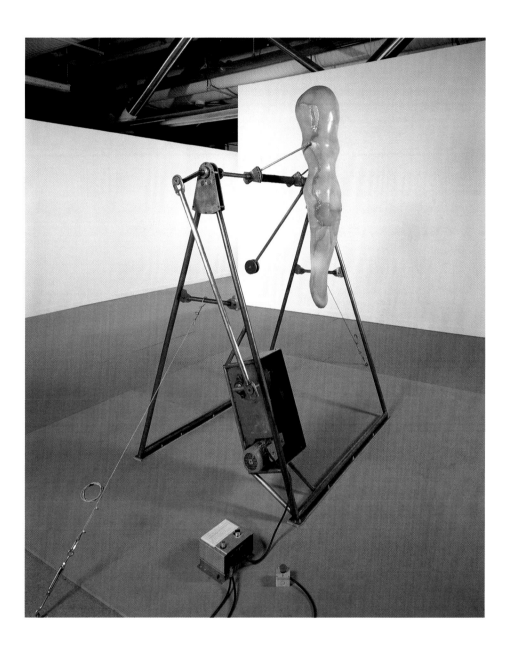

∧
Marie-Ange Guilleminot
Saint-Germain-en-Laye, 1960
La Rotateuse
(The Rotator /
Rotating Woman)
1995

Resin, gum drop,
various materials
217 x 170 x 157 cm
Purchased 1996
AM 1996-321

without taking into account what went before, albeit eschewing the notion of progress. The second, by combining progress in materials and techniques, tends to identify progress in science and technology with progress in art. One cannot, of course, sum up the two tendencies as implying, on the one hand, an artistic future dependent on history or, on the other, a future developing oblivious of the present, because the distinction is never so clear cut, and the tendencies sometimes overlap. And it would be vain to speculate on the forms that 'contemporary art' will take in the years ahead.

Although it is not invariably so, it is certainly true that genres and practices complement each other, flow into each other, and develop through cross-fertilisation, to the point that the very concepts of sculpture and painting no longer seem adequate for describing contemporary art. And it is true that for many contemporary artists, these terms do not correspond to their work or their techniques, and they deliberately avoid using them. Other artists feel that, on the contrary, painting and sculpture have always developed by pushing back the limits of their media, to the extent that they have ended up absorbing photography, painting, video and film, often trans-forming them into tools of investigation and works that unquestionably do belong to the history of painting and sculpture.

The figures of Gilles Barbier (*Polyfocus*), for example, are undeniably part of the history of sculpture and the representation of the body in particular, which was doubtless the most widespread theme of the second half of the twentieth century, and one which saw the renewal of a fundamental branch of what we can only call 'sculpture'. Here the age-old question of resemblance – an issue that has been discussed in theoretical writings since Greek Classical sculpture –comes to the fore. Plaster casts of living bodies, as well as wax, resin, and silicon, have made it possible to achieve an astonishing degree of realism (it too conventional), a realism all the more striking because it goes hand in hand with technological and scientific advances in this domain. Incorporating a living body into a performance, as in the work of Roman Signer (*Bottes / Boots*), leaving traces of the body, in a literal way, in certain elements (traces of the artist's feet inside a pair of boots) or in a work's relation to the floor (which is merely the result of past actions) in fact relates to an archaic sculptural practice – that of the artist leaving his mark in the material. Such works bear witness

^

Gilles Barbier
Port-Vila (Vanuatu), 1965
Polyfocus
1999

Wax, fabric, rubber and various materials
Variable dimensions
Purchased 2000
AM 2000-30

Roman Signer
Appenzell (Switzerland), 1938
Bottes (Boots)
2000-2001

Steel, rubber, carbon dioxide,
acrylic paint
Variable dimensions
Purchased 2001
AM 2001-46

v
Xavier Veilhan
Lyon, 1963
The Rhinoceros
1999-2000

Resin, polyester, varrnish
110 x 140 x 415 cm
Purchased 2001
AM 2001-26

to the permanence of an artistic form practised internationally since the 1950s, one which consists of combining an action or bodily movements (sometimes involving the public) with different objects that bear witness, once the performance is over, to the processes which governed its genesis. For sure, these remnants of the action are not necessarily the essential elements of the work, but their palpable materiality is sometimes more than a simple document or the residue of a non-renewable act that has disappeared. The physical presence of the object, the concretisation of the material actually engenders, secretes as it were, a sculptural space. When the viewer is confronted with Xavier Veilhan's *Rhinocéros*, he or she is confronted, first and foremost, with a piece of sculpture. The work clearly harks back to the nineteenth-century tradition of animal sculpture, with its fondness for exotic animals and lyrical settings. Slightly larger than its living model, this animal, finished in a bright industrial colour, is above all a massive object placed in the very space occupied by the spectator. It is a large form which expresses ways of relating to space based on such sculptural considerations as scale, volume, dimension, the perception of colours and the reflection of light.

<
Jean-Marc Bustamante
Toulouse, 1952
Site II
1992

Steel, lead, wax, enamel
470 x 390 x 43 cm
Purchased 2001
EC 2001-68

∧
Erwin Wurm
Bruck an der Mur
(Austria), 1954
One Minute Sculptures

48 colour prints
Each 30 x 45 cm
Purchased 2000
AM 2001-7 (1-48)

The photographs of Erwin Wurm in the series *One Minute Sculptures* are an example of the permeability of media and the shifting of sculptural considerations to a new realm, since these pictures derive simultaneously from photography, performance and sculpture. They show people carrying out an action which consists of striking a pose, sometimes difficult and absurd, for around one minute often with the aid of everyday objects, thereby attempting to create situations which imitate numerous recent sculptures. For Erwin Wurm, this kind of photography is really a form of sculpture; these are not simply images which record the ephemeral. This approach is slightly reminiscent of the importance that photography had for sculptors such as Medardo Rosso and Constantin Brancusi, who photographed their own works after having arranged them.

This photographic dimension of sculpture is also a feature of the work of Jean-Marc Bustamante (*Site II*), and not merely because he likes to present his photographs and sculptures together. Bustamante seeks to fix, to crystallise materials, traces and temporalities, to make them part of the sculptures as if to enable something that no longer exists to reappear. This photographic aspect of sculpture is another way of revealing certain emotions and perceptions – which could possibly come from photographs of trees and or landscapes close to cities – or revealing materials, as if mental or physical images appear in them.

The work of Ugo Rondinone (*The Evening Passes Like Other. Men and Women Float Alone*) incorporates moving images in strange volumes, reminiscent in form and colour of little clouds, which in turn seem to be moving but which also in turn transmit their massive static forms to the pictures. The four screens show continuously four different images (a man opening a door or a car coming over the horizon, for example) and the music is always the same, so that the volumes, through their weight and their immobility, become like a three-dimensional part of the images and sounds.

∨
Ugo Rondinone
Brunnen (Switzerland), 1963
The Evening Passes Like Other. Men and Women Float Alone
1998

Various materials + 4 video tapes + 1 audio cd
100 x 100 x 45 cm
Purchased 2000
AM 2001-37

Two other video artists, Peter Fischli and David Weiss, use a strong materialisation of everyday objects to give an unusual dimension and presence to things that are so much a part of everyday life that we no longer see their physical properties. Through the colours and unexpected materials used, these objects appear larger and heavier, more imposing. It is precisely through the change in scale, the materials used, their uniform volume highlighting their form and structure that they acquire status as sculptures.

The display cabinets of Gabriel Orozco (*Mesas de trabajo / Work Tables*), featuring various everyday objects transformed by the artist, also draw on a source of inspiration that could not be simpler – the reality of the surrounding world – but this time the factual and

v
Peter Fischli
Zurich, 1952
David Weiss
Zurich, 1946

Kerze (Candle)
1986-1987
AM-2001-8

*Besteckbehälter
(Cutlery Holder)*
1987
AM-2001-14

Wurzel (Root)
1987
AM-2001-12

Napf (Ladder for Dog)
1986-1987
AM-2001-9

Mauer (Wall)
1987
AM-2001-13

Hocker (Pouffe)
1987
AM-2001-11

Elastomere
Variable dimensions
Purchased 2000

∧
Gabriel Orozco
Veracruz (Mexico), 1962
Mesas de trabajo
(Work Tables)
1990-2000

Various materials
Variable dimensions
Purchased 2001
AM 2001-46

the everyday are raised to a higher aesthetic level. Placed in display cases like rare objects, they are more like objects from a contemporary cabinet of curios than images, forms, materials, words, scraps of concepts or sketches, all kinds of thoughts given concrete form by the author which appear as so many future sculptural projects. The world thus becomes a kind of reservoir of sculptures and thoughts.

Nevertheless, the multiplicity of the most recent contemporary artistic practices defies the concepts and ideas which make it possible to analyse sculpture and painting. When all is said and done, we have three options: we can accept the concepts of painting and sculpture, we can reject them, or we can juggle the two. But these positions are not so simple when we seek to define, with regard to these same works, what painting and sculpture are or could be. No doubt the quest for the essence of painting or sculpture is less interesting or relevant than works of art, because what is interesting and relevant about such works is the very fact that they push back the boundaries of a possible definition or essence.

Index

(The figures in italics refer to illustrations.)

Photographic credits

Photoengraving
Offset Publicité, La Varenne Saint-Hilaire

Printing
Mame Imprimeurs, Tours (n° 01102214)

Dépôt légal
December 2001

A Creativ̶ ̶ ̶ ̶ ̶ ̶ ̶ ̶ c

Teac̶ inc̶

A Creative Approach to Teaching Spelling

The what, why and how of teaching spelling – starting with phonics!

by Kate Robinson

BLOOMSBURY

LONDON · OXFORD · NEW YORK · NEW DELHI · SYDNEY

Bloomsbury Education

An imprint of Bloomsbury Publishing Plc

50 Bedford Square	1385 Broadway
London	New York
WC1B 3DP	NY 10018
UK	USA

www.bloomsbury.com

Bloomsbury is a registered trademark of Bloomsbury Publishing Plc

First published 2016

British Library Cataloguing-in-Publication Data

A catalogue record for this book is available from the British Library.

ISBN:
PB 978–1–4729–2245–8
ePub 978–1–4729–3012-5
ePDF 978–1–4729–3011-8

Library of Congress Cataloging-in-Publication Data

A catalog record for this book is available from the Library of Congress.

10 9 8 7 6 5 4 3 2 1

Typeset by Newgen Knowledge Works (P) Ltd., Chennai, India
Printed and bound in India by Replika Press Pvt. Ltd.

Contents

Introduction

Approaches to teaching spelling have evolved greatly over the last decade. There is a fresh understanding of the value of phonic knowledge in developing and improving reading and spelling. Phonic skills are now a key component of most spelling programmes. It is nonetheless widely recognised that phonic skills alone are not enough to develop confident spellers.

This book explores the current research on teaching spelling with phonic and other strategies and summarises the successful approaches. It goes on to introduce a broad range of games and other fun activities that employ these approaches. Games can be selected to meet the needs of particular pupils or the challenges of specific word groups. With additional guidance on assessment, selecting words to learn, creating multi-activity spelling sessions and spelling at home, teachers can enhance existing programmes or develop their own spelling programmes to meet the specific needs of pupils.

1
Spelling: the what, why and how

Why teach spelling?

'Why do we all need to spell the same way?' asks Simon Horobin, Professor of English Language and Literature at the University of Oxford (Horobin, 2013, p. 1). It is a question worth asking, particularly by those teaching or learning spelling. Conventional spelling is highly prized in education, in the workforce and throughout society. Weak spelling is seen by many, often erroneously, as indicative of weak communication skills generally and, more broadly, of low educational standards. In a 2012 survey, poor spelling is cited by employers as one of the primary reasons for rejecting job applications: 'Our employers highlight poor spelling and grammar as the key cause of rejection' (StudentGems, 2012, p. 1).

However misguided attitudes to non-standard spelling might sometimes be, there are good reasons to value both an agreed spelling convention and spelling that adheres to it. For readers, spelling that follows an agreed and recognised convention is easier and quicker to decipher than spelling which does not. For writers, a clear, agreed spelling convention, and the ability to follow it, allow them to represent their meaning without the distraction of having to consider which spelling option to choose. Nonetheless, there's no doubt that for those who struggle to learn conventional spellings, the experience of writing can be stressful and debilitating. Every thought strains towards remembering or guessing spellings, or towards adapting language choices. It is hard to hold onto meaning if you are constantly grappling with how to spell each word.

When we help pupils to spell, we are helping them towards a complete freedom of written expression with which their full intellectual capacity can be unleashed. The confident speller can allow thoughts, memory and imagination free rein to engage with the subject matter and to be expressed fully through written words. In a world where personal, social and political power are so closely linked to communication, this freedom, or lack of it, can have immense consequences for individuals.

Changing attitudes and approaches to the teaching of spelling

Pre-1970s

Before the 1970s, spelling was largely taught by introducing children to graded lists of words to memorise. These lists were most often grouped alphabetically, by theme or completely randomly. Teachers highlighted errors for children to correct and learn (Westwood, 2014). Shlagal (1998) describes the introduction of simple memorising techniques and some attempts to organise words according to their spelling patterns. Few other cognitive strategies for learning were used. From the 1950s to the 1970s, the ideas of linguists such as Noam Chomsky (1975) and psychologists such as Jean Piaget (1955) and Lev Vygotsky (1978) were sowing the seeds for a radically different strategy that was to take shape during the 1970s: the 'Whole Language' approach.

1970s–2000s: The Whole Language approach

The belief emerged that the best way to help pupils develop language skills was simply to introduce inspiring, creative learning activities that were anchored in the pupils' own experience and personal aspirations, or to allow pupils themselves to formulate such activities. It was thought that this would best encourage each pupil's innate motivation to use and develop their language skills. The teaching of specific knowledge and skills should be incidental – a response to a pupil's immediate need as they were reading, writing, speaking or listening – rather than planned and structured formally into lessons.

Indeed, Frank Smith, a leading proponent of the Whole Language approach, wrote: 'My own recommendation for how reading and writing should be taught is perhaps radical; they should not be taught at all' (Smith, 1994, p. 229). In addition, many believed anyway that the English spelling system was simply too complex to allow for a formalised, structured approach to teaching spelling. Hence, from the mid-1970s through to the early years of the twenty-first century, many pupils were not taught spelling (or other distinct language skills such as reading and grammar) in a formal or structured way.

2000–present

In the last two decades there has been mounting concern about the standards of spelling in schools and in society at large. In addition, evidence against the Whole Language approach has steadily grown:

After half a century of advocacy associated with instruction using minimal guidance, it appears that there is no body of sound research that supports using the [Whole Language] technique with anyone other than the most expert students. Evidence from controlled experimental studies almost uniformly supports full and explicit instructional guidance rather than partial or minimal guidance for novice to intermediate learners. These findings and their associated theories suggest teachers should provide their students with clear, explicit instruction rather than merely assisting students in attempting to discover knowledge themselves.

(Clark, Kirschner and Sweller, 2012, p. 11)

There has also been a growing appreciation of the degree of regularities within the English spelling system. David Crystal tells us:

It has been estimated that only about 3 per cent of everyday English words are so irregular that they would have to be learned completely by heart, and that over 80 per cent are spelled according to regular patterns. That leaves some 15 per cent of cases where we could argue the status of their regularity. But given such statistics, the chief conclusion must be that we should not exaggerate the size of the problem . . .

(Crystal, 2003, p. 272)

In consequence, the past two decades have seen profound developments in how we teach spelling and reading, with the explicit, structured teaching of synthetic phonics emerging as a key strategy.

Phonics

Phonics for spelling and reading

A **phoneme** is a distinct unit of sound, such as the **'sh'** sound in the spoken word **'fish'**.

A **grapheme** is the single letter, or the group of letters, that we use to represent each phoneme in writing – such as the letters **s** and **h** together for the **'sh'** sound.

Phonic skills include those needed to:

1   Segment, or split, a spoken word into individual phonemes, recall which graphemes represent each phoneme and then write them in the correct order to spell the word.

2   Identify all the distinct graphemes in a written word, recall the phonemes that they represent and then to mentally or orally blend these phonemes together in order to read the word.

There is now a wide body of evidence showing that teaching phonic skills early in children's education has a substantial impact on the development of reading ability (Ehri *et al.*, 2001). The evidence to show an additional impact of phonic skills on spelling ability is now also strong (Mann, Bushell and Morris, 2010).

Of great influence was the UK government's review in 2006, led by Sir Jim Rose, the Independent Review of the Teaching of Early Reading. Here, following a far-reaching analysis of the available evidence, Rose stated categorically that 'the knowledge, skills and understanding that constitute high quality phonic work should be taught as the prime approach in learning to decode (to read) and encode (to write/spell) print' (Rose, 2006, p. 71). The development of phonic knowledge is highlighted as a key early strategy in the UK government's Primary National Curriculum for English (Department for Education, 2013).

Synthetic and analytic phonics

Two different approaches to developing and using pupils' phonic skills have emerged.

- In **synthetic phonics**, the initial and primary strategy used for *reading* is to identify each grapheme in a written word (**sh o p**), to recall each of the phonemes, or sounds, they represent and then to blend the phonemes together into a spoken word. The initial strategy for *spelling* is to hear each separate phoneme, or sound, in a spoken word, to recall the graphemes that represent each of these phonemes and then to string the graphemes together into a written word.
- In **analytic phonics**, the primary strategy is for pupils to compare whole spoken or written words to find similarities in their phonemes or graphemes. From these similarities, pupils deduce how to read or spell unfamiliar words.

The majority of studies suggest that, of the two approaches, synthetic phonics has the most significant impact on pupils' progress in reading and spelling. Rose reports:

The practice seen by the review shows that the systematic approach, which is generally understood as 'synthetic phonics', offers the best and most direct route to becoming skilled readers and writers.

(Rose, 2006, p. 4)

Most of the phonics programmes now used in schools, such as Jolly Phonics, Letters and Sounds and Read Write Inc., use synthetic phonics as the key strategy. For most pupils, the development of the skills needed to distinguish each of the individual phonemes in a spoken word, and then to recall the individual graphemes that represent them, needs to be a key component of their spelling programme. In this book, many of the games and activities, and the multi-activity spelling session, include the development of these synthetic phonic skills.

The difference between reading and spelling

Spelling is more difficult than reading because phoneme-letter relations are more inconsistent than letter-phoneme relations . . .

(Bosman and Orden, 1997, p. 9)

When we read a word, there is a relatively limited number of possible sounds that each grapheme might represent – often just one possible sound and only occasionally more than two. Therefore, when reading, we generally only have to choose between a small number of phonetically viable pronunciations of a written word. Take, for example, the written word **wade**: each of the three graphemes, **w**, **a_e** and **d**, only have one commonly associated phoneme that they are likely to represent. Therefore there is only one phonetically viable way to pronounce the whole word: basic phonics training will allow a pupil to accurately read this word.

By contrast, when we spell a word, many sounds can be represented by two, three and often many more possible graphemes. So there are often a large number of phonetically viable spellings for the same word. Imagine the same pupil trying to spell the spoken word **'wade'**. Phonetically viable spelling options for this word could include **wade**, **whade**, **waid**, **whaid**, **weighed** and **wheighed**: lots of room for mistakes if phonic training alone is relied on. Furthermore, when reading, once we have identified the phonetically viable pronunciations of a written word, we can then employ our knowledge of vocabulary, semantics and syntax to further filter out words that are nonsense words or do not make sense in the given context. These factors do not, however, help us to choose the spelling of a word.

2
Phonics plus

While ample evidence points to the key role that phonics should play in spelling programmes, it is widely agreed that, both for reading and spelling, phonetic skills alone are not enough to ensure success. Here, we will look in more detail at some of the issues, particularly those relating to spelling, and how they can be addressed.

Sub-lexical sound-spelling correspondences

'The br**ight** l**ight** in the n**ight** sky gave me a fr**ight**'

Since the emergence of phonics as the primary initial strategy for developing basic reading and spelling skills, there has been some dispute about whether, as well as teaching pupils to recognise and recall individual grapheme-phoneme correspondences, we should also be helping them to recognise and recall longer, commonly occurring, patterns in words. These patterns, sometimes referred to as 'sub-lexical sound-spelling correspondences', are groups of phonemes or graphemes that frequently occur in a recognisable string within words. Examples are common consonant clusters – **pl**, **str** – and common word endings – **ate**, **ight**, **orn**, **eer**.

The concern among some is that if we focus on helping pupils read and spell these sound clusters, or strings, rather than ensuring that they are confident at identifying the correspondence between individual phonemes and graphemes, then pupils will not develop the vital skills and knowledge needed to break down and build up words from their individual graphemes or phonemes. Hepplewhite, for example, writes:

My observations of [slower-to-learn] children is that given a diet of being taught consonant clusters as specific units of sound such as 'sp', 'st', 'str', 'sk' and so on, they can sometimes be inaccurate as to 'which' cluster the word has. It is the SKILLS of blending all-through-the-printed-word and segmenting all-through-the-spoken-word which need to be extremely well-taught – rather than an emphasis on teaching consonant clusters as if they are little bits of code 'knowledge'.

(Hepplewhite, 2011, p. 1)

However, she does acknowledge that proficient readers are most likely to 'apply "chunk" phonics – perhaps at "syllable chunk" level such as "sta-tion", "sun-set", "foot-ball" and "Con-stan-ti-no-ple"'. The case for sometimes focusing on these larger word parts when teaching spelling is strong. Westwood argues that the ability to remember common word parts, or 'chunks', is actually a key stage in the development of spelling skills:

When a pupil begins to recognise and use commonly occurring groups of letters that represent key parts of words rather than relying on single letter encoding, even more English words become easier to spell . . . Over a period of time, young learners must begin to store and remember visual images of common letter sequences that represent pronounceable parts of longer and more complex words – sequences such as: str-, pho-, gra-, pre-, tion, eet, -eal, -ally . . .

(Westwood, 2014, p. 4)

Jolliffe *et al*, in their guidance for teaching synthetic phonics in primary schools, agree:

As children's phonic knowledge develops and they become more confident about synthesising phonemes, they can begin to cluster or 'chunk' letters more easily, which will help them to read more quickly and spell more accurately.

(Jolliffe, Waugh and Carss, 2012, p. 63)

Reliance on individual grapheme-phoneme correspondences alone cannot deliver complete accuracy. In addition, it can become slow and cumbersome. Learning to recall and use clusters of graphemes that represent strings of phonemes can help pupils to address the limitations inherent in using individual grapheme-phoneme correspondences to spell.

As teachers, we can work to ensure that pupils have a thorough understanding of grapheme-phoneme correspondences, and that they can segment and blend words at the level of single phonemes and graphemes, while also helping to extend and broaden their skills by introducing and reinforcing longer patterns. Many of the games introduced in this book provide opportunities to focus on larger word parts as well as on individual phonemes and graphemes.

Morphology

magic   magical   magician

A morpheme is the smallest unit of meaning in a language. The word **magical** consists of two morphemes – the root word **magic** and the suffix **al**. Morphology is the study of these units of meaning. Spelling programmes which include morphology improve spelling. Nunes, Bryant and Barros (2012) report on various intervention studies that show improving children's awareness of morphology has a positive effect on their reading and their spelling. Nunes and Bryant (2006) explain in detail why the teaching of morphology helps spelling. Some key factors are:

- Many morphological units do not follow predictable letter-sound correspondences and so phonological knowledge alone cannot guide spelling. (E.g. **ed** is used for the past tense of regular verbs but can be pronounced **'t'** as in kiss**ed**, or **'d'** as in kill**ed**. An understanding of the meaning and uses of the morpheme **ed** will help to ensure accurate spelling whatever the pronunciation.)

- The addition of an affix can change the pronunciation of a root word, in which case an awareness of the root word will support accurate spelling (e.g. magi**c**/magi**c**ian).

An exploration of the morphology of words, looking at root words, the affixes we can attach to them and the meanings of different root words and affixes, can help pupils to understand the impact of meaning on spelling and to use association by meaning to support their spelling.

> In this book, Games 11, 12 and 13 help pupils to develop their morphological knowledge and to apply this knowledge when spelling. Appendix 1 lists a range of common affixes and their meanings to support such morphological games and activities.

Rules

'i before e except after c'

frie**nd**   re**cei**ve   an**cie**nt ???

Spelling 'rules' are attempts to explain in words a pattern in English spelling. Many of our spelling rules are extremely complex. For example:

[When] adding suffixes beginning with vowel letters to words of more than one syllable: If the last syllable of a word is stressed and ends with one consonant letter which has just one vowel letter before it, the final consonant letter is doubled before any ending beginning with a vowel letter is added. The consonant letter is not doubled if the syllable is unstressed.

(Department for Education, 2013, Appendix 1, p. 11)

In addition, the majority of spelling rules have a number of exceptions or qualifying conditions. Furthermore, many pupils struggle to learn when focusing on abstract principles. Kolb and others have highlighted the benefit of making concrete experience a key part of the learning cycle (Kolb, 1984).

For many pupils experiencing a pattern – exploring, seeing, hearing, associating and analysing a set of words that follow that pattern – is a more effective learning strategy than simply memorising an explanation, or rule, for the pattern. The rule can be used to back up and reinforce these other strategies. Most of the games and activities in this book can be used in conjunction with, or instead of, rules, to highlight and reinforce spelling patterns.

> Games 16 and 17 look specifically at how rules can be used with other strategies to learn particular patterns.

Association

Many of the strategies described above draw on a further key strategy, that of ***association***. By associating together groups of words that have the same pattern – that follow the same 'rules', have the same grapheme-phoneme correspondences, the same root word or the same affix – we reinforce pupils' awareness of the pattern, their ability to recall the graphemes that form the pattern and also their ability to transfer their knowledge of the pattern to new words.

In addition to simply grouping words that follow the same pattern, we can employ a range of further strategies to highlight and reinforce the association. Silly rhymes, songs, sentences and wordplay, pictures and even drama can all help pupils to build word associations and hence develop their knowledge of spelling patterns. For words ending in 'ould' you could use the following mnemonic.

For most of the games in this book, words are grouped by pattern in order to support the use of association when recalling spellings. Games 14 and 15 help teachers and pupils to further enhance the association between words, using pictures and silly sentences. Appendix 2 gives further examples of sentences that can be used to associate groups of words that have the same pattern.

Multisensory approaches

In the past, much credence has been given to the theory that pupils have precise and varied individual 'learning styles', each of which responds best to a specific form of stimulus, such as visual, auditory or kinaesthetic. However, in recent years the evidence supporting this theory has been shown to be weak (Coffield *et al.*, 2004; Stahl, 2002; Pashler *et al.*, 2008). There is, though, a growing body of research showing that teaching and learning approaches which are multisensory, incorporating visual, auditory, kinaesthetic and tactile elements, have more success than uni-sensory approaches. Shams and Seitz concluded from their analysis of available research that:

Multi-sensory training can be more effective than similar uni-sensory-training paradigms . . . . In general, we conjecture that perceptual and cognitive mechanisms have evolved for, and are tuned to, processing multisensory signals. Under such a regime, encoding, storing and retrieving perceptual information is intended by default to operate in a multisensory environment, and uni-sensory processing is often sub-optimal as it would correspond to an artificial mode of processing that does not use the perceptual machinery to its fullest potential.

(Shams and Seitz, 2008, p. 5)

We have evolved to process information being received through a number of senses at the same time. Hence, signals that only use one sense limit our processing potential. Further studies have suggested that multisensory approaches are particularly useful for teaching reading and spelling and for pupils with learning difficulties (Cook, 2011; Phillips and Feng, 2012). The Rose review states that, 'Phonic work for young children should be multisensory in order to capture the interest, sustain motivation and reinforce learning in imaginative and exciting ways' (Rose, 2006, p. 71).

The majority of the games and activities in this book are multisensory, asking pupils to engage in a range of visual, auditory, kinaesthetic and tactile approaches within one activity. Games 19 and 20 combine the use of touch and feel with visual and auditory approaches. The specific value of further sensory approaches is considered below.

Movement

Learning activities that involve movement can help to engage pupils and stimulate learning. Jensen (2005) describes a range of brain functions that are improved when movement is integrated into learning. Most obviously:

Oxygen is essential for brain function, and enhanced blood flow increases the amount of oxygen transported to the brain. Physical activity is a reliable way to increase blood flow, and hence oxygen, to the brain.

(Jensen, 2005, p. 62)

Outlining a broad range of research, Jensen concludes that 'a solid body of evidence shows a strong relationship between motor and cognitive processes' (Jensen, 2005, p. 71). He describes in particular evidence that stimulating the vestibular (inner ear) through movements such as jumping, bending, spinning and rolling can result in 'significant gains in attention and reading' (Jensen, 2005, p. 71). More recently, Shoval has undertaken further research into the possible impact of movement on learning. She describes how movement *requires* pupils to engage in an activity in a way that passive learning does not. Her study led her to conclude: 'The more the learners used learning activities with movement, the higher their academic achievements' (Shoval, 2011, p. 462). Furthermore, physical movement can often be instrumental in creating a fun learning experience. When learning is fun, it is engaging and memorable. Hence, when fun physical activities are used appropriately, so that they enhance rather than distract from the key learning goal, they can promote learning.

> Many of the games in this book involve movement beyond handwriting, such as manipulating cards and props. Games 3, 4, 6, 9 and 21 involve more energetic gross motor movements, such as walking, running, throwing and catching, to engage pupils and stimulate cognitive activity.

Mouth movements

Montgomery reports on some children with dyslexia making dramatic improvements in spelling when they use 'multisensory mouth training'.

This involves asking the pupil to articulate a letter sound such as 'l' and then describing where in the mouth the key articulators are touching. E.g., 'Where is the tip of your tongue now? Are your lips open or closed? Feel your voice box, what is it doing?' And so on.

(Montgomery, 2012, p. 120)

She explains that, 'If the dyslexic does not have the awareness of the articulatory "feel" of a particular phoneme it will make the sound-symbol association particularly problematic to acquire' (Montgomery, 2012, p. 120). A significant number of pupils benefit from focused attention on the changes in the position of key articulators (e.g. lips, tongue, teeth), as different phonemes are vocalised. For some, these physical sensations are easier to distinguish and then to associate with a visual symbol (grapheme) than are the auditory signals of phonemes.

> Game 22, Mouth Awareness Game, helps pupils to develop awareness of these sensations and to associate them accurately with graphemes.

Handwriting

Writing a word involves a series of tiny fine-motor movements. When remembering how to write a word, part of what a pupil is recalling is the sequence of fine-motor movements needed for that word. Handwriting that is slow or awkward can inhibit this memory process (Berninger, 2012). The confident use of cursive writing, in which a word is one continuous, unbroken pattern of movements, can actively help pupils to remember spellings (Montgomery, 2012). Games and activities that support the development of confident cursive handwriting, and which help pupils to retain a memory of the particular physical movement involved in spelling a word, can be useful for many.

> In this book, Game 23 is a fun, laughter-inducing activity that helps pupils to attend to, and memorise, the physical sensation of writing a word.

Further approaches for tricky words

Many commonly used words do not follow a common pattern of grapheme–phoneme correspondence. (Some examples are **to**, **my**, **their** and **people**.) This can make them particularly challenging to learn to spell. Such words are often described as 'tricky words'. In addition, some words that do follow a more common pattern can still prove hard for some pupils, requiring additional, specially selected strategies to support learning. For such words, and such pupils, a range of further approaches can be employed. Many have been included in the games and activities that follow. Some examples of these approaches are:

- Identifying words within words:

  w**here**

- Identifying and highlighting tricky bits:

  fr**i**end

- Pronouncing words as they are spelt:

  pe *o* ple   wed *nes* day

- Mnemonics (wordplay):
  because:

  ***because* b**ig **e**lephants **c**an **a**lways **u**nderstand **s**mall **e**lephants

  necessary:

  It's ne**c**e**ss**ary to have **one C**ollar and **two S**leeves on a shirt.

- Pictures (to highlight a visual shape or pattern):

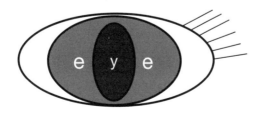

Game 18 shows how these approaches can be embedded into a fun spelling activity for tackling tricky words.

Look Say Cover Write Check (LSCWC)

Look Say Cover Write Check is one title given to a popular method for helping pupils to memorise spellings. In its simplest form, the method involves practising spelling by looking at a written word, saying it, covering it up, writing it and then checking if it is correct. This is repeated, with a group of words, a few times during a week. Various tables, such as the basic example below, have been developed for this activity.

Word	Try 1	Try 2	Try 3	Try 4

LSCWC is often used in conjunction with a weekly spelling test: words are practised for a week and then tested towards the end of the week. Frequently, children are expected to use this method at home with family support in preparation for weekly spelling tests.

A wide body of research indicates that the LSCWC method improves spelling ability (e.g. Fisher, Cozens and Greive, 2007; Jaspers *et al.*, 2012). It is primarily a visual method, asking pupils to focus actively on memorising the visual appearance of a word. For this reason, some suggest that it is only appropriate for use with trickier words that cannot easily be encoded by recalling grapheme–phoneme correspondences. However, it's worth bearing in mind that, as we have seen, many words have more than one phonetically viable spelling which pupils have to choose between. So, even where the correct spelling is phonetically regular, pupils can benefit from visual strategies such as this, as well as other strategies discussed, to help them recall which phonetically regular alternative is right. In addition, many versions of the technique have been developed that allow for a range of other strategies, including phonetic or morphemic analysis, to be integrated into the strategy, benefiting from and enhancing the visual techniques and the repetition.

Below is a table for a version of this method that incorporates a few possible additional strategies. Words to practise are given in the 'Word' column and a tip to aid memory is given in the next column. The tip can involve highlighting a pattern, tricky bit or word inside the word. It can involve splitting the word into graphemes or longer word parts, or perhaps giving a mnemonic or picture.

Ou for the short /u/ sound

1. _Read_ the silly sentence.
2. _Say_ the first word in the word column, and the tip.
3. _Write_ the word in the 'Write and Trace' column.
4. _Trace_ over your written word with your finger or the end of a pen.
5. _Cover_ up the word and try to write it again.
6. _Check_ if it's right.
7. _Practise_ again or repeat with the next word.

Silly Sentence

The **c**o**u**ple of **y**o**u**ng **c**o**u**sins were **d**o**u**ble tr**o**uble

Word	Tip	Write and Trace	Try 1	Try 2
couple	c **ou** p le	_couple_	_couple_	_couple_
double	d **ou** b le	_double_	_double_	_double_
trouble	t r **ou** b le	_trouble_	_trouble_	_trouble_
cousins	c **ou** s i n s	_cousins_	_cousins_	_cousins_

Further additional strategies that can be incorporated within a basic Look Say Cover Write Check approach can readily be found online. In this book, Chapter 8 demonstrates how the LSCWC method can form a useful part of multi-activity learning sessions.

Revisiting

Most pupils need to revisit new words, or sets of words, a number of times before they are able to remember how to spell them. The LSCWC method is one way of structuring repetition and revisiting into spelling programmes. Another way is to focus on the same group of words for a number of sessions, exploring the words through varied games and activities over time. Guiding pupils towards practising words at home, with family support, is another commonly used way to ensure pupils are revisiting words. LSCWC is often used to enable this as, given appropriate initial guidance from teachers, family members generally find the process straightforward to follow (see Chapter 9). Another way to help pupils revisit words is to encourage them to use newly learnt words, and words learnt in the preceding months, in their writing, as discussed below.

Dictionaries and spell checks

Dictionaries and spell checks are no substitute for becoming a proficient speller. However, they can support editing and improve spelling. Successfully searching for a spelling in a dictionary, or choosing between word choices offered by a spell checker, requires active, engaged analysis of the grapheme–phoneme correspondences in a word. This act of analysis can aid memory.

> Activities that develop the skills needed to use dictionaries and spell checks well, and that help pupils to value and enjoy the process of using them, can be useful. Game 27 is an example of such an activity.

Spelling in context

Our final aim is to increase the number and range of words that our pupils are able to use confidently and accurately in their writing. The accurate use of new words in writing will itself help pupils to retain those words into the future. But the leap from writing words in a spelling learning activity to choosing to use them freely in writing can be a difficult one, requiring an additional level of confidence and ability. So an important part of a spelling programme is activities that encourage and support pupils in using new words in their writing.

> In this book, Games 24 and 25 encourage pupils to use newly learnt words in their writing.

Self- and peer-editing

Independent, successful spellers are able to reflect on the spelling in their writing and to notice and attend to words that don't seem right. For many who struggle to spell, this reflective and corrective process is particularly hard, sometimes due to an understandable reluctance to confront mistakes and sometimes because the necessary reflective and analytical skills are undeveloped.

Successful self-editing of spelling requires pupils to feel an active ownership of their writing and, in addition, to have some clear strategies for questioning and remedying spelling. We can encourage pupils to ask themselves questions such as, 'Does this word look right?', 'Do the graphemes match all of the sounds that I can hear in the word?', 'Are there words with the same sound, that I learnt with this one, that I remember?' and 'Could I find this in a dictionary?'

Well managed peer-editing can provide a useful step towards self-editing. For many, the knowledge that peer-editing is going to take place can itself improve performance by motivating pupils to reflect and self-edit as they write.

Games and activities that teach self- and peer-editing in a fun and non-threatening way can help pupils to embed these skills into their independent writing practices.

> Game 26 in this book is one example of how pupils can be encouraged and helped to edit spelling.

3
Summary of key current approaches to word analysis for spelling

As we have found, there is general agreement that synthetic phonics should be at the heart of our approach to teaching spelling, but that good spelling programmes need to build on this with a range of further strategies. Here is a summary of the current approaches already described and how they could be applied to a word or group of words:

- **Phonics:** highlighting each individual grapheme–phoneme correspondence

b r ea th i ng

- **Sub-lexical sound–spelling correspondences:** highlighting letter strings that represent common phoneme strings

br ea th **ing**

- **Morphology:** attending to the individual units of meaning within a word, including root words, prefixes and suffixes

breath ing

- **Rules:** describing patterns in English spelling. An example is, 'When adding a suffix that starts with a vowel to a root word that ends in two consonants together, just add the suffix straight on without changing the root word'

brea**thing**

- **Association:** grouping and associating words with the same pattern

Ca**tch** the cat!
He's out of the ki**tch**en
Into the hu**tch**
To sna**tch** a rabbit
For tea!

- **Multisensory approaches:** using a combination of visual, auditory, kinaesthetic and/or tactile strategies to support learning

- **Handwriting approaches:** focusing on the physical movement involved in writing words

breathing

- **Approaches for tricky words:** choosing from a range of further strategies to help memorise the tricky part or the whole word

Because . . . .

Big **e**lephants **c**an **a**lways **u**nderstand **s**mall **e**lephants

- LSCWC

Silly Sentence				

*The c**ou**ple of y**ou**ng c**ou**sins were d**ou**ble tr**ou**ble*

Word	Tip	Write and Trace	Try 1	Try 2
couple	c **ou** p le	*couple*	*couple*	*couple*
double	d **ou** b le	*double*	*double*	*double*
trouble	t r **ou** b le	*trouble*	*trouble*	*trouble*
cousins	c **ou** s i n s	*cousins*	*cousins*	*cousins*

- Further strategies for reinforcing and embedding learning including dictionary usage, revisiting, spelling in context and editing.

Most pupil groups, and many word sets, will benefit from a combination of these strategies. The games, activities and multi-activity spelling session that follow are examples of how the strategies can be used individually and in combination to engage pupils and respond to a wide range of pupil needs and word types.

4
Introducing how we spell to pupils

As they engage in games and activities for spelling, pupils will begin to develop an *implicit* understanding of how words are built and of the varied ways in which they can help themselves to remember spellings. A question for teachers is how *explicit* we make this knowledge. Should we help pupils to understand and reflect on the processes and strategies involved in the activities that they undertake? And should we help pupils to understand and use specific linguistic terminology associated with spelling – for example, words such as phoneme, grapheme, morpheme, suffix and prefix?

Processes for word building and strategies for spelling

The National Curriculum in England requires that pupils do have an understanding of *the process* of spelling:

The process of spelling should be emphasised: that is, that spelling involves segmenting spoken words into phonemes and then representing all the phonemes by graphemes in the right order.

(DfE, 2013, p. 20)

It also calls for pupils to have a clear understanding of how words are built, for example requiring that:

pupils should continue to be taught to understand and apply the concepts of word structure so that they can draw on their knowledge of morphology and etymology to spell correctly

(DfE, 2013, p. 36)

In Chapter 5, 'Assessment and self-assessment', we consider how pupils' own analysis of their spelling performance, and of spelling learning activities, can enhance their learning. To fully undertake such analysis, pupils need an explicit understanding of the processes and strategies they are using when they learn to spell new words. Games and activities that include explicit exploration of the processes involved are likely to enhance pupils' ability to engage with, and assess, performance and activities.

Terminology for spelling

The National Curriculum in England encourages teachers to introduce pupils to vocabulary that will help them analyse language:

Throughout the programmes of study, teachers should teach pupils the vocabulary they need to discuss their reading, writing and spoken language.

(DfE, 2013, p. 5)

Whilst some required vocabulary is listed in the Grammar and Punctuation Appendix of the National Curriculum in England, many words relevant to reading and spelling words, such as 'grapheme' and 'phoneme', are not specifically mentioned. Nonetheless, many teachers do employ a range of spelling-related terminology with even young primary aged children. Having a precise common language with which to discuss and analyse words and spelling processes aids learning. Waugh, Warner and Waugh assert that: 'A shared meta-language allows teachers and children to talk together using terms that everyone understands' (Waugh, Warner and Waugh, 2013, p. 11).

The more precise the terminology that pupils are able to use, the more detailed and precise their analysis and understanding can be. So, for example, a pupil who understands not just the term 'grapheme', but also 'digraph' and 'trigraph', is better placed to precisely identify, categorise and remember the range of graphemes in words being learnt. If such terms are introduced gradually and positively, in context and when useful, with lots of repetition, they can quickly become an empowering tool that pupils use with ease.

> A number of the games in this book support the easy introduction of spelling terminology. See, for example, Game 8.

5
Assessment and self-assessment

When planning an assessment process, we need to consider exactly why we are assessing, what precisely we need to assess and what we intend to do with the information gathered. These will all inform how best we should assess.

Well-crafted spelling assessments can help us select the most appropriate word groups for pupils to learn. They can also help us understand which strategies will best build on the strengths highlighted and which strategies will respond best to the learning needs revealed.

Why are we assessing spelling?

In answering this question, it's worth stressing first what we are *not* doing when we assess spelling – we are not teaching. Formal spelling tests, as well as worksheets and activities that test knowledge without explicitly supporting learning, can too easily become the main content of a spelling programme. While such activities can play a part in helping to reinforce teaching and learning that has taken place, they need to remain in a subsidiary role to focused imaginative teaching and learning activities if pupils are to learn and progress well.

Nonetheless, in order to select the most appropriate words for pupils to learn, and the most appropriate strategies with which to support learning, we do need to assess which words, sub-lexical units and graphemes pupils are using successfully and which they are making mistakes with. We need to know if pupils are recalling and using words learnt and if the strategies and activities that we have chosen have helped or hindered their learning. We need to know how well pupils are progressing in relation to their previous achievements and also in relation to the class curriculum and the national curriculum.

We must bear in mind that such information is only of use if it informs our ongoing practice within a full planning, teaching, learning and assessment cycle. The content and strategies in future spelling sessions must build on the information gathered from spelling assessment activities.

What are we assessing and what will we do with the information gathered?

Assessment can offer us a broad picture of the stage pupils are at in their spelling development, as well as a more precise understanding of their specific spelling achievements and difficulties.

Understanding and responding to pupils' stages in development

Experts have defined four or five stages in the development of a person's spelling skills (e.g. Frith, 1985; Gentry, 2011). Westwood (2014) describes the following:

Stage 1: Pre-phonetic (also referred to as 'pre-communicative' stage)

At this stage, which is typical of children aged three to five, a child 'plays' at producing writing in imitation of the writing of others, using a random mix of capital letters and shapes. There is no connection between these scribbles and speech sounds or real words.

Stage 2: Phonetic

At this stage, which typically emerges at age six years, the child relies mainly upon phonemic awareness and a beginning knowledge of letter-to-sound correspondences. Even without instruction, the words children invent at this stage are often quite recognisable, because they are applying aspects of the alphabetic code that they have acquired incidentally. Naturally, many inaccuracies exist at this stage because the spelling of many English words is not entirely predictable. Toward the end of this phonetic stage, the approximations move much more nearer to regular letter-to-sound correspondences.

It should be noted that the majority of older individuals with poor spelling have reached this phonetic stage but have not progressed beyond it. Their problem is a tendency to be over-dependent on phonic information, and therefore they write all words as if they have perfect letter-to-sound correspondence. They need to develop more effective ways of processing and remembering words visually in order to build up a store of correct orthographic images.

Stage 3: Transitional

At approximately seven to eight years old children reach a stage where there is clear evidence of a more sophisticated understanding of word structure. The child becomes aware of within-word letter strings and syllable junctures, and is better able to use memory for word images to check what has been written. The children who gain real mastery over spelling at this stage also begin to use words they know already in order to spell words they have never written before (spelling by analogy).

Stage 4: Independence

This stage is achieved by eight plus years in normally developing children, but much later in students with learning difficulties. At this stage children have mastery of quite complex phonic principles and strategies, and use visual imagery effectively when writing and checking familiar words. But even at this stage, spellers still make some errors. Independent spellers are good at self-monitoring and make flexible use of a range of spelling, proofreading and self-correcting strategies.

One value of assessment is that it can help us to understand which of these stages pupils are in, so that we can identify any radical divergences from typical progress and respond, where necessary, with further focused assessments and interventions. It also allows us to offer pupils activities and strategies geared to the needs of the stage they are in. While these stages will necessarily overlap, we can broadly say, with regard to spelling, the following:

- Pupils in Stage 1, the pre-phonetic stage, will benefit from activities that promote a general interest in the written word and help to develop their fine-motor and letter-formation skills.
- Pupils in Stage 2, the phonetic stage, are ready for activities that develop their phonic skills and their knowledge of grapheme–phoneme correspondences.
- Pupils in Stage 3, the transitional stage, are ready for spelling activities that focus on larger word parts and whole words.
- Pupils in Stage 4, independence, are ready for activities that develop their understanding of complex phonic and morphological principles and rules and help them to employ a range of strategies to edit their own work successfully.

Understanding and responding to individual progress and needs

To gain a more precise picture of how each pupil is progressing, there is a range of information that we can gather about their spelling that can inform our future teaching practice. Although many mistakes can be categorised in a number of different ways, it is nonetheless useful to analyse mistakes where possible. Such analysis helps us to address mistakes appropriately and also to recognise emerging patterns in mistakes that may need particular interventions. Table 5.1 lists key issues, along with examples and possible responses to these issues.

Table 5.1

Issue	Examples	Possible responses
How many spelling mistakes? (e.g. in a spelling test)	7 mistakes out of 10	If high, consider the number and difficulty of spellings given. May also need to question strategies employed
What spelling mistakes?	**maek** for **make**	Re-teach words in new way
Are there patterns to the kinds of mistakes, such as:		
• Particular spelling patterns	**horribel** for **horrible** and **terribel** for **terrible**	Re-teach the grapheme–phoneme correspondence or longer pattern with fresh strategies
• Particular parts of words	suffixes (e.g. **comeing** for **coming**)	Appropriate morphological activities Re-teach pattern/rule in new way
• Rule not understood	**peice** for **piece**	Re-teach rule in new way
• Letter order muddled	**strenght** for **strength**	Further develop knowledge of particular grapheme–phoneme correspondences Consider visual and kinaesthetic strategies

• Sounds omitted or completely misrepresented (no grapheme–phoneme correspondence)	**song** for **strong** **bit** for **big**	Build phonic analysis skills Further develop knowledge of grapheme–phoneme correspondences Consider visual, kinaesthetic and other non-phonic strategies
• Phonetically viable alternative spellings offered	**hed** for **head**	Further develop knowledge of grapheme–phoneme correspondences Consider visual strategies
• Not using morphological knowledge	**magisian** for **magician**	Appropriate morphological activities
How is the letter formation and handwriting?	Non-cursive handwriting Illegible handwriting Poorly formed letters	Consider handwriting development activities Tactile and handwriting games and activities
What strategies or games are successful?	Physical games (e.g. ball games)	Extend use of identified games or activities
What strategies or games are not being used at all?	No dictionary usage No self-editing	Consider whether to re-introduce strategy or, if not appropriate for this pupil, highlighting alternative strategies

How should we assess?

Spelling tests

Traditionally, pupils have been given weekly word-list spelling tests – word lists that they have had opportunities to learn and are then tested on. There is ongoing debate about the value of such spelling tests, particularly for pupils who struggle to spell well. Key arguments that have been made against weekly spelling tests include the following:

- They are de-contextualised – they do not assess spelling in a realistic context and therefore do not give an accurate picture of how well a child can recall and spell words in a real-life writing context.
- They are not testing how well a child retains and uses words from previous weeks, only from the current week.
- Information from them is not used in any meaningful way.
- Words selected and tested do not relate to each child's interests and learning needs.
- Poor achievement in spelling tests is demoralising.

As Waugh, Warner and Waugh highlight:

For some children, the mark they achieve in the Friday spelling test can cause anxiety, frustration and a sense of failure. It can compound their sense of being a poor speller.

(Waugh, Warner and Waugh, 2013, p. 48)

However, as Gentry (2011) argues, well managed spelling tests can be 'the most efficient way for a teacher with a room full of students to find out if your child already knows a pattern or weekly unit of words'. Such tests can provide valuable information about pupil progress and about teaching methods used. They can also motivate children to learn spellings. If we are to use them, however, we need to address the issues raised: word-list tests should only form one part of our assessment process. Other activities, as described below, need also to be assessed in order to give a more thorough body of information.

Word tests and other assessments should focus on the range of words learnt in previous weeks and months, not just the current week's words, so that recall and usage of spellings over time is monitored. All evidence from assessments needs to become part of a focused planning, learning and assessment cycle, informing future planning and teaching. Word lists should be differentiated as much as is feasible within a large group, so that each small group is learning words that match their abilities, needs and interests. For some children, individual word lists may be required. Perhaps most importantly, we must always remember that the teaching given prior to tests is key to learning.

Spelling tests do not just have to take the form of word lists. They can also be developed as sentence dictations and proofreading activities that include the set words.

Reviews of free writing and learning activities

As discussed, spelling tests alone will not give us a full picture of a pupil's progress and needs. Certain issues, such as which strategies are helping them, will only be apparent if we observe them as they undertake free writing or spelling learning activities. In addition, pupils perform differently in tests to free writing. Hence the inclusion of free writing and spelling learning activities in our assessment process is vital if we are to gain a full picture of our pupils.

Discussion and self-assessment

Further useful strategies include discussions with pupils and pupil self-assessment. Through discussions we can illicit which strategies pupils find most useful and we may gain insights into issues that we were unaware of.

Self-assessment activities are another way for us to gain insights into a pupil's preferences and difficulties that may not be apparent in their writing. They can also encourage pupils to take ownership of their learning, evaluating their successes and their mistakes, the reasons behind them and possible further action needed. There is much evidence that this kind of active role in the learning process enhances achievement (Prince, 2004; Michael, 2006).

Self-assessment can range from simply marking one's own tests, through self-editing, to undertaking a careful analysis of one's own learning and mistakes. We can guide pupils' self-assessment by following up learning and assessment activities with spoken or written questions, appropriate to the activity and to the understanding and ability of the pupil. Table 5.2 lists some possible questions to support self-assessment of spelling in different contexts.

Table 5.2

Self-assessment of spelling tests
What was my result?
What helped me learn the words that I got right? (*some possible answers can be offered* – 'already know them / LSCWC / liked the games we played / other:_____ ')
What did I find difficult about the words I got wrong?
What would help me to learn these words?
Self-assessment of a spelling learning activity
Am I more confident about the words we practised?
Did the activity help me learn the words?
What did I like or dislike about the activity?
Self-assessment of a free writing activity (before or after editing/marking)
Which words am I most pleased that I used?
Are there any words that I think might be spelt wrong?
What did I do if I wanted to write a word that I wasn't sure how to spell?
Which words would I most like to practise?
How would I like to practise these words?

Such questions can be given on a follow-up sheet to be completed after selected activities or they can be the basis for verbal discussions. Pupils will need ongoing support to understand the diverse range of possible answers to such questions and to answer with reflective, insightful detail.

Gathering, collating and applying assessment information

Having looked at the types of activity that can be included in spelling assessments, and at the types of questions that can be brought to bear on these activities, we can consider appropriate formats for gathering, collating and then applying assessment information. The content and ease of use of the format will impact on how well we utilise the information gathered.

Teachers need to decide how regularly they are going to record assessment information. Many will wish to gather information from all test activities and then from other activities at regular intervals. Below is an example of a record sheet that can be used to gather, record and plan responses to such information. It allows for progress against specific targets to be monitored closely over time. It provides for the analysis of broader issues, such as successful and unsuccessful strategies, and for planning actions that respond to the evidence gathered.

Spelling assessment record sheet					
Name					
Year group: 1				**Stage:** 2 (Phonetic)	
Notes from previous record sheet *Good memory for spelling during varied learning games and tests.*	**Date / Assessment Activity**	*Spelling test 1/2/15*	*Spelling learning game 20/2/15*	*Class writing activity 10/3/15*	*Spelling test 22/3/15*
Pattern / word set		✓ - used correctly		✗ - used incorrectly	0 - not tested/ used
/n/ sound spelt n before k (-bank, chunk etc)		✓	0	✗	✓
tch (catch, fetch etc)		0	0	0	✓
/v/ sound at end of words (-have, give, cave etc)		0	✓	✗	✓
Successful strategies / Current issues		*Not applying spelling knowledge when free writing*			
Action needed		*Try Spelling In Context activities, e.g. 'Who's This?'*			

When a pupil displays serious difficulties with spelling, for example falling well behind the typical stages of development or showing a pronounced pattern in the number or type of errors made, a more detailed Assessment Record Sheet can be used. In this, questions from Tables 5.1 and 5.2 can be included in a detailed, individualised spelling error analysis that informs a personalised programme of support.

The strategies, games and activities outlined in this book are designed to help teachers successfully support all pupils, particularly those who struggle to learn to spell. In addition, further detailed and focused guidance is available for those teachers who are offering personalised spelling assessment and support programmes to pupils with dyslexic-type difficulties (e.g. Phillips, Kelly and Symes, 2013; Kelly and Phillips, 2011; Stansfield, 2012).

Selecting words to learn

Assessment activities can give us specific information about which patterns and words pupils can spell, which they are making mistakes with and which they are not using at all. When selecting a word or group of words for pupils to learn, teachers need to consider various additional factors, including:

- **How useful are these words to this pupil group?** Do pupils understand the meanings of these words and do they use them already when speaking? Do pupils already know how to read these words? Have they tried to use them in their writing? If not, are pupils likely to use these words in their writing? Words that are meaningful to pupils and which are readily used in speech and free writing are easier to learn and remember.

- **How straightforward are the grapheme–phoneme correspondences within the words?** Are the spelling patterns in these words simple and/or common, or are they complex and/or uncommon? Table 5.3 classifies some key spelling patterns and considers their comparative difficulty to pupils.

Table 5.3   Key spelling groups

Single letters representing single sounds ***These are particularly easy to hear and spell in CVC words***	Single letters that represent a single sound will generally be easier to remember than more complex grapheme–phoneme relationships. e.g. the **b** in **b a t** *CVC words are three-letter words that begin with a single **c**onsonant, have a single **v**owel in the middle and a single **c**onsonant at the end. Each sound is quite distinct and easy to hear and is represented by only one letter.*
Consonant digraphs	Graphemes made of two consonant letters that represent one sound: **sh**op, lo**ck**. These are a little harder to recall than a single-letter grapheme, as two separate shapes (letters) need to be recalled for each sound.

Consonant clusters	Two or more consonant graphemes that are next to each other in a word. Each grapheme retains its own sound: pl gr phr shr str Many pupils initially find it hard to hear and process each distinct sound in consonant clusters. Lots of careful, clearly pronounced phonic work, highlighting each distinct sound and matching it to the correct grapheme, is often needed when first learning to spell a new consonant cluster.
Vowel digraphs	Vowel digraphs are groups of two vowel letters that represent one sound: r**ai**n. It can be very hard to remember which vowel or vowel digraph represents which sound, as many vowel sounds can be represented in a wide variety of ways. Take, for example, the long vowel sound /ā/ in the following words: **a**corn, c**a**p**e**, r**ai**n, pl**ay**, v**ei**n, n**eigh**bour, th**ey**, st**ea**k. Many pupils need a variety of additional non-phonic strategies to learn the spelling of words with vowel digraphs.
Silent letters	Silent letters are letters that are not pronounced. They usually indicate an old pronunciation that is no longer used. They are often 'tied' to another letter: **k**not, **g**nat, cas**t**le. As they are not heard, there is no phonic clue in the spoken word reminding us to use them. A range of strategies may be required to learn them.
Trigraphs and quad-graphs	Trigraphs are groups of three letters that represent one sound: h**igh**. Quad-graphs are groups of four letters that represent one sound: thr**ough**. Like consonant digraphs, trigraphs and quad-graphs are generally harder to recall than one-letter graphemes.
Affixes ***Affixes that make no change to the spelling of the root word*** ***Affixes that change the spelling of the root word***	Affixes are morphemes – word parts that carry a single unit of meaning – that are added to root words to change the meaning of the word. Most common are prefixes, which are added to the beginning (e.g. **un**do, **re**turn) and suffixes, which are added to the end (e.g. help**ful**, happi**ness**). Spelling words with affixes is easiest when the affix has no impact on the spelling of the root word (e.g. cat**s**, match**es**, hard**est**). Spelling words with affixes is harder when the affix causes a change to the spelling of the root word (e.g. <u>babi</u>**es**, <u>mak</u>**ing**, <u>hopp</u>**ing**). Many 'rules' have been developed to guide pupils in these spellings, some useful, some complex and full of exceptions. Often other strategies, such as association, can play a key part in helping pupils learn these spellings. These issues are discussed in more detail in the section on Rules in Chapter 2, Phonics plus.
Uncommon grapheme–phoneme correspondences	Some quite commonly used words include a grapheme–phoneme correspondence (GPC) that is uncommon – a group of letters that is only used to represent that particular sound in a very few English words: b**eau**tiful, m**au**ve. The rareness of these GPCs means that words containing them can be harder to learn.

Further key issues when selecting and grouping words

Table 5.4

Homophones	A homophone is a word that is pronounced the same as another word but differs in meaning, and may differ in spelling. For example, **there**, **their** and **they're** are homophones. Such words are often taught together. However, I want to bring a note of caution to this strategy: associating words together that we *don't* want pupils to mix up can increase the confusion. Instead, try teaching these words at different times, so that no confusing association is created. Where possible, associate each word in a set of homophones with words that *do* follow the same spelling pattern. Alternatively, where a word is alone in following a particular grapheme–phoneme correspondence, use a tricky word activity, or other focused activity, to highlight and teach a specific spelling.
	their heir to the throne **here, there** and everyw**here**   **you're** happy, **we're** happy, **they're** happy 
Grapheme strings that have the same pronunciation but different spellings	Some words contain word parts that have the same pronunciation, but a different spelling, to corresponding parts of other words: offi**cial** and ini**tial**; assist**ant** and independ**ent**. The spellings of such words are easily confused. In some cases, rules or morphemic analysis can help pupils to recall the appropriate spelling pattern, although there are almost always exceptions to such guidance. Again, for many pupils, learning such spelling patterns at different times can help to limit the confusion. Additional strategies, such as exaggerated pronunciation or saying words 'as they are spelt', can also help.

Grapheme strings that have a similar, but slightly different, pronunciation but different spellings	Some words contain word parts that have a similar, though slightly different pronunciation, to a corresponding part of another word that is spelt differently: mea**sure** / pic**ture**; bo**th**er / o**ff**er.
	Bringing together these words with close but distinct grapheme–phoneme correspondences, through games and activities that encourage pupils to carefully compare and contrast the sounds and graphemes with which they are built, can help to highlight the distinctions. Game 10 helps pupils to notice and respond to subtle differences in the sounds within words.

We have discussed the benefits of associating words with the same spelling–sound correspondences. In England, Appendix 1 of the English Programmes of Study, within the National Curriculum, is a detailed table of spelling patterns to be addressed from Year 1 to Year 6 and it gives a number of examples of words that follow each pattern. Building on the expectation that some straightforward grapheme–phoneme correspondences will have been learnt previously, during the Early Years Foundation Stage, the table generally orders patterns well, in terms of technical difficulty and likely usefulness for different age groups. Within the English Programme of Study table, a few patterns are grouped together that, as indicated in my table above, some pupils may find easier to learn separately.

In this book, Appendix 2 gives further examples of sentences and pictures that can be used to associate groups of words with the same pattern.

6
Selecting and preparing games

The games in Chapter 7 have been arranged into categories to help you select those that are most appropriate to your pupil group and to the patterns and words you are focusing on. You may wish to consider whether IT resources could enhance your chosen games. How you and your pupils articulate the whole words, word parts and individual phonemes that you are focusing on will also impact on the success of a game. These factors are explored further here.

Selecting games

When choosing which games to use, you will need to consider the type of pattern in the words you are currently focusing on. For example, if it is a simple grapheme–phoneme correspondence, you may find games from the first section 'Written words' useful, along with games in the 'Word association' section. If the words are linked by a common prefix or suffix, you may find games in the section 'Morphological analysis' more appropriate. Words that do not fit easily into any pattern, or which your group are really struggling to learn, may require games from the 'Tricky words' section.

You will also need to consider how familiar the words are to your group. This will affect whether you need to use games that start with written or with spoken words. Clearly, words and word parts that are written give explicit information about a word's spelling, which is useful if any of the grapheme–phoneme correspondences are being taught for the first time. However, pupils need to work towards independently hearing and identifying the separate phonemes in spoken words and recollecting the graphemes that represent them. The first section of games, 'Written words', starts with analysis and study of the written words or word parts and then moves towards helping pupils recall graphemes from the spoken words. The second section of games, 'Spoken words', focuses more quickly on using the spoken word to trigger recollection of graphemes. These games are appropriate with words that have already been introduced to pupils. When you are ready to check recall of previously practised words, and to encourage their use in writing activities, games from the 'Revisiting and editing' section are useful.

How can computers enhance spelling games?

Many pupils are comfortable with keyboards, mice and screens, associating such resources with fun and games. Some, particularly those who struggle with writing, associate pen and paper with stress and failure. With spelling, as with many learning activities, tablets and PCs allow work to be edited or scrapped without leaving a trace behind, which, for many, is liberating. Interactive whiteboards and large screens can aid large-group work. Furthermore, computer-based games can easily be saved and adapted for future use. A range of phonic-based spelling software packages are available to purchase. These can provide useful individual practice opportunities for pupils.

A number of the games in this book can easily be adapted for use on large or small screens. Using software such as PowerPoint, Active Primary, or Smart Notepad, simple text boxes can replace word-cards; images and shapes can be reproduced. Pupils and teachers can drag such objects into appropriate positions as games require.

Articulation

It is common, when articulating individual phonemes, to inadvertently add an additional sound /ə/, to the end of the phoneme. This sound is known as 'schwa'. It is the sound represented by the grapheme **er** in the word sist**er**. So, for example, when pronouncing the phoneme represented by the single-letter grapheme **m**, we might mistakenly say 'mer' (or 'mə'), instead of 'mmm'. This is confusing for pupils. It suggests the presence of a phoneme, with a corresponding need for a grapheme, which actually isn't there.

All the games and activities provided here involve, at some stage, clearly articulating the word to be spelt and often carefully highlighting the phonemes from which the word is built. It is important that when doing this we do not include unnecessary schwa sounds. There are now a number of good videos online that show how to pronounce accurately the 44 different phonemes in the English language.

Presentation

The visual features of a game can help to make it more enticing. They can also actively support learning by highlighting aspects of words or groups of words. Colour, font, font size, bold print and a range of other formatting tools, along with pictures, diagrams and layout, can all be used to promote learning. Many of these are demonstrated within the descriptions of the games in Chapter 7. Colour is one that has not been possible to include here but is well worth using when available.

7
Games and activities for spelling

Here you will find a wide range of games and activities based on the principles and strategies described in this book. For guidance in selecting appropriate games for your pupils, see Chapter 6.

Written words

Game 1: Grappling with Graphemes

Summary

Pupils split written words into the graphemes that represent each phoneme. They then recall and write each grapheme independently.

Resources

For each small group:

- A list of a few words with a common pattern
- Some blank A4 card or an A4 whiteboard for each pupil

Activity

Teach: The whole group looks at the first word on the list. The group recalls how to read the word and practises reading it slowly so that each phoneme can be clearly heard. Highlighting each phoneme in turn, the group decides which letters build each of the graphemes that correspond with each phoneme.

Practise: Split the large group into smaller groups of pupils that correspond in size to the number of graphemes in each of the additional words – a three-person group for a word with three graphemes, a four-person group for a word with four graphemes, etc.

Assign each group a word appropriate to the group size. Ask each group to identify together each grapheme in their word, with each pupil copying one of the graphemes onto their whiteboard. Now ask each group in turn to show their whiteboards to the class, each pupil waving their grapheme, and shouting out the phoneme it represents, in the right order.

Apply: Clean all of the whiteboards and hide the word lists. How many groups can now rewrite their graphemes and reshow their words? Can anyone rewrite the whole word given to their group? Can anyone rewrite another group's word?

Game 2: Words on Pictures

Summary

Pupils build words from graphemes or larger word parts.

Resources

For each pupil:

- A background scene on a sheet of paper, for example a bare tree, an underwater scene or a train engine
- A set of words with a common pattern, split into individual graphemes. Cards in a shape that complements the background scene are ideal – e.g. leaves, fish, carriages etc.

- Some blank grapheme cards

For large-group work:

- A larger set of the same grapheme cards

Activity

Teach: Tell pupils one of the words in the set. Pronounce the word slowly and clearly, emphasising each phoneme. Discuss which grapheme might represent each phoneme.

Practise: Explain which grapheme is common to the set of words. Discuss other words that might have the same grapheme. Give a background scene and a set of grapheme cards to each pupil. Can pupils sort the grapheme cards into words on the scene?

Apply: Having discussed and read through the words and their graphemes carefully as a group, who can now turn their scene over and recall and write the words that they have built on their scene?

Follow-up activity: On a consecutive spelling session, give pupils fresh copies of the same resources, but this time with some grapheme cards left blank. Can pupils now fill in the blank grapheme cards and rebuild the words on the scene?

Variations

Words can be split into larger sub-lexical units or morphemes. For example, words ending in **ture** could be split: **cr–ea–ture, fur–ni–ture, pic–ture, na–ture, ad–ven–ture**. If splitting words into these larger sub-lexical units, it's important that, when asking pupils to recall the graphemes or string of graphemes that represent the word part, we still carefully sound out each phoneme. This helps pupils to continue to use and develop their knowledge of grapheme–phoneme correspondences.

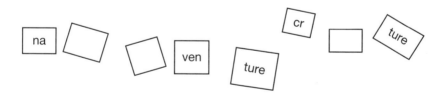

Game 3: Word Part Relay

Summary

Pupil teams compete in a relay race to be the first to gather all the graphemes, or larger word parts, for a given word.

Resources

For each pupil team:

- A set of three words with a common pattern, split into individual graphemes on card

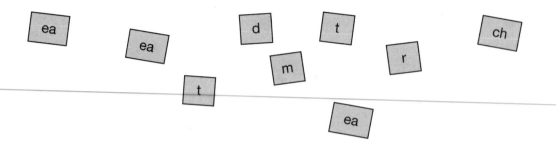

Preparation

Organise the pupils into small teams of two to four. Place all of the grapheme cards onto a table at one end of the room. Clear some space in front of the table and make a start line.

Activity

Teach: Gather the whole group around the table, or ask them all to look at the graphemes displayed in text boxes on the interactive whiteboard. Tell the pupils one of the words in the set. Pronounce it clearly, emphasising the individual phonemes. Can the pupils suggest the graphemes that are likely to represent the phonemes? Can they now find the grapheme cards on the table/whiteboard?

Practise: In their teams, pupils stand behind the start lines. Clearly tell the pupils another word from the set, again emphasising the phonemes. Ask one pupil from each team to go to the table, find the first grapheme and then return it to the next pupil in their team. This pupil must find the next grapheme, returning both to the next pupil in their team. Teams continue until all graphemes are found. The winning team is the team which is first to hold the correct grapheme cards up in the right order. Repeat with the third word.

Apply: Label each team A or B. Now the A teams must think of a word that follows the same pattern for the B teams, and vice versa. You can whisper a word to any team that struggles to think of one. Teams now segment their word, recall the appropriate graphemes and write each one onto a blank card. Place all of the newly written graphemes on the table. Now first the B teams and then the A teams are told their words. They race to see which teams can gather all of their word parts first and then hold them up in the right order.

Variations

When appropriate to the word set or pupil group, words can be split into larger sub-lexical units or morphemes. See 'Variations' for Game 2.

Game 4: Treasure Hunt

Summary

Pupils hunt for hidden graphemes, or larger word parts, to build into words.

Resources

- A set of words with a common pattern, each word split into graphemes on cards. Have one set for each pair of pupils and a further set for you.

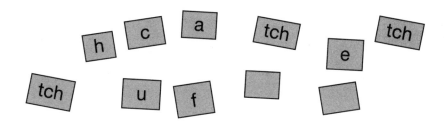

- Some blank word-part cards and a few filled in with random graphemes not related to this set of words.

Preparation: Hide each pair's grapheme cards for two words around the classroom.

Teach: On the whiteboard or a table that everyone can see, have some grapheme cards, among which are the graphemes for another word in your set (not the words hidden around the room). Say the word you are looking for, sounding out the phonemes very clearly – **'h–u–tch'**. As a group, search for the grapheme cards needed to represent each grapheme and put them in the right order.

Practise: Explain that more word-parts are hidden around the classroom. Say another word clearly, verbally highlighting the phonemes. In pairs, pupils discuss what phonemes they can hear and what grapheme cards they need to find. They then hunt for the grapheme cards around the room. Repeat for another word.

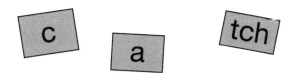

Apply: Ask the whole group to identify the common grapheme–phoneme pattern in the words already found. Now ask each pair to think of another word with the same pattern and practise splitting it into graphemes. Once their graphemes have been checked by you, pairs write them on blank cards and hide them around the classroom. They then tell another pair to seek for the word they have hidden, carefully sounding out the word. Repeat with another word.

Game 5: Kim's Game

Summary

Words are split into sub-lexical units on cards which are placed on a tray and hidden under a cloth. One word-part card is sneaked away and the cloth is pulled off. Can pupils identify and spell out the letters on the missing word-part card?

Resources

- A set of words with a common pattern split into sub-lexical units on cards

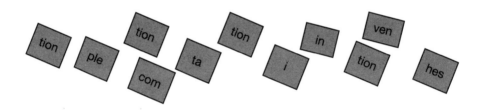

- A tray
- A cloth
- Some blank word-part cards

Activity

Teach: Place the word-part cards for one word on the tray in a random order. Ask the whole group to look at the tray and see if they can work out the word on the tray. Once it's been recognised, look closely at each sub-lexical unit together and discuss the grapheme–phoneme correspondences and any other noticeable features.

Practise: Place the cloth over the tray and sneak away one word part. Who can identify and spell out the missing word part? Repeat with the other word parts, asking one or all pupils to spell out each missing word part in order. Repeat with some of the other words in the set.

Apply: Can any pupil choose either a word already covered or a new word from the set to split into word parts on the blank cards and use to lead a round of Kim's Game?

Variations

- Instead of sneaking away a card, rogue cards can be snuck in. Can pupils identify the word part that does not belong to the word being displayed?
- Words can be split into individual graphemes or morphemes.

Game 6: Skittles

Summary

Words are split into sub-lexical units that are attached to skittles. Pupils knock down as many skittles as they can and then see how many words they can build from those knocked down. They then try and recall the spellings of those words.

Resources

- A skittles set
- A set of words with a common pattern, split into sub-lexical units on cards

Activity

Teach: Explore the set of words on the board with the group, carefully examining the grapheme–phoneme correspondences, common patterns, meanings and any useful morphological features.

Practise: Attach the sub-lexical units of three or four of the words to the skittles. Pupil teams take turns to see how many of the word parts they can knock down and then sort into words. Each team is then given a short time to re-examine the spelling of the words on the skittles before the skittles are whisked away and they try to accurately write down the spelling of their words. The skittles are then replaced for the next team. The winning team is the team that accurately spells the highest number of words.

Apply: Who can spell out the word parts of words already used, or of new words with the same pattern, onto cards to stick onto the skittles for another round of the game?

Spoken words

This section of games focuses more closely on helping pupils to hear each phoneme in a spoken word and then recall the graphemes that represent those phonemes. The first three games can be used with a wide variety of word sets, particularly word sets that are being revisited. The final game, 'Listen Close', is useful where words have similar but not identical sounds represented by different graphemes.

Game 7: Grapheme Stick Man

Summary

Like the game Hangman, pupils offer word parts to build up a word, trying to guess the complete word before it's too late. However, in this case the gallows of Hangman are replaced with a stick man and the word parts are not just individual letters but graphemes – letters or letter combinations representing individual phonemes.

Resources

- A large board

Preparation

Select a previously practised set of words with a common pattern for revisiting.

Activity

Teach: Choose one word from the set and draw a horizontal line for every grapheme in the word.

_____   _____   *(for **ea ch**)*

Tell the group the sound of the common word part (in this case the phoneme /iː/) but do not tell them the spelling (in this case **ea**). See who can recall graphemes for this sound. If graphemes other than **ea** are offered, add a line to the stick man:

Practise: Once **ea** has been recalled, ask pupils to consider what other graphemes could go with **ea** to make a word. If graphemes other than the one intended (in this case **ch**) are offered, add additional lines to the stick man:

If the group completes the word before the stick man is complete, they've won. If not, you've won! Now try with other words from the set.

Apply: Can anyone in the group recall another word from the set with which to lead a game of Stick Man?

Game 8: We're Going on a Grapheme Hunt

Summary

Pupils listen carefully to the phonemes in words and write down the graphemes that they think represent them. They then consider what types of grapheme they are and feed them to the right grapheme 'bear'.

Resources

- Three boxes, labelled 'single-letter grapheme (1 letter)', 'digraph (2 letters)' and 'trigraph (3 letters)'. (These boxes can also be decorated as bears.)
- Blank pieces of paper

Preparation

Select a set of words with a common pattern, which the group has already practised, to revisit.

Activity

Teach: Tell the group that you are going on a grapheme hunt to hunt for graphemes to feed to a hungry family of bears. If the pupils are familiar with the popular children's book *We're Going on a Bear Hunt* (Rosen and Oxenbury, 1989), you can sing an adapted version of the refrain:

We're going on a Grapheme Hunt.

We're going to catch a big one.

What a beautiful day!

We're not scared.

Sound out one of the words from the set you have selected, clearly articulating each phoneme (e.g. **'r–igh–t'**. Sound out the first phoneme and see if anyone can write it down. Show the boxes to the group and discuss their labels. Discuss which box (or 'bear') should gobble up the grapheme and then ask a pupil to pop it in. Write the grapheme on the board.

Practise: Slowly articulate the word again. See who can identify the next phoneme and write down the corresponding grapheme. Can they select the right 'bear' to be fed with this grapheme?

Repeat with the rest of the phonemes in the word, writing a copy of each grapheme onto the board. When you have completed a word, review the graphemes on the board and recall which box each went into.

Now try with some other words in the set.

Apply: When you have completed two or three words in the set, ask the group to recall the pattern that was common to all the words. Can any member of the group recall another word from this set to carefully sound out so that other group members can try and recall the correct graphemes?

Game 9: Catch

Summary

In pairs, pupils pass a ball, taking it in turns to identify a phoneme and then recall the corresponding grapheme, in a word.

Resources

- A ball for each pair of pupils

Preparation

Select a set of words with a common pattern, one that the group has already practised, to revisit.

Activity

Teach: Sound out one word in the set, clearly articulating each phoneme. Can the group identify and say each phoneme in the set? Ask a volunteer to throw the ball to you, saying each phoneme in turn. As you return the ball each time, you spell out the letters in the grapheme that represents that phoneme.

Practise: Now ask the pupils to repeat this in their pairs, one identifying the phonemes and the other recalling the graphemes.

Introduce another word in the set. Can pupil pairs segment the word into phonemes and recall the graphemes? Some pairs may prefer to identify phonemes and graphemes slowly together first and then practise recalling while throwing the ball.

Apply: When pairs have practised two or three words in the set, ask the group to recall the pattern that was common to all the words. Can any pair recall another word from this set to segment and recollect corresponding graphemes, while playing catch?

Variations

- Words can be also split into larger sub-lexical units for partners to spell out.
- Other ball games, such as goal scoring or shooting the hoop, can be adapted for practising spellings in this way.

Game 10: Listen Close

Summary

This game is useful for words containing phonemes or sub-lexical units that sound *almost, but not quite, the same* as another phoneme/word part. In these cases, extra careful pronunciation and listening are the key to choosing the correct grapheme. Some examples of such graphemes are:

- the phonemes represented in the suffixes **s** and **es**
- the phonemes represented by the graphemes **f** in **if** and **th** in **this**
- the phonemes represented by the graphemes **o_e** in the word **hope** and **o** in the word **hop**.

Pupils listen closely to spoken words and wave in the air the correct grapheme for use in that word.

Resources

- For each member of the group and the teacher: two large grapheme cards, one for each of two easily confused word parts
- Small whiteboards or blackboards, or a few blank word-part cards, for each member of the group

Activity

Teach: The whole group looks at each of the two word-part cards in turn, and carefully and accurately pronounces the two different phonemes or phoneme strings.

Practise: Hold both your cards behind your back. Randomly pull one out at a time and see if all learners can say the correct phoneme. Now randomly call out one or other of the phonemes and see if all the pupils can hold up the correct card.

Apply: Call out whole words with one or other of the phonemes in them. See if the pupils can correctly hear the phoneme and hold up the correct grapheme card.

Now with the mini whiteboards or blank cards to hand, see if learners can correctly *write* the graphemes for each phoneme when you call out a phoneme. Next, can they write a whole word containing one of the phonemes when it is called out?

Variations

- Instead of having two cards for each pupil, choose two opposite classroom walls, and label each with one of the graphemes. Pupils have to choose which wall to run to when you call out a word.
- Longer sub-lexical units can also be compared, such as **ible** and **able**.

Morphological analysis

Game 11: Lucky Dip

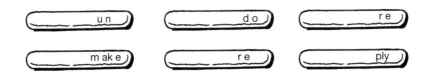

Summary

Pupils join affixes to word roots to build new words and explore their meanings.

Resources

- Two trays of sand
- Some lolly sticks
- Dictionaries

Preparation

Choose two or three suffixes or prefixes to focus on. Write each one on the base of a few lolly sticks and stick them, word parts hidden, into one of the trays of sand. Choose a number of root words, each of which can be matched with one or two of the suffixes or prefixes. Write these onto further lolly sticks and plant them in the other tray of sand.

Activity

Teach: As a group, pick a root word from the root word sand tray and discuss if it has a clear, independent meaning when it stands alone. For example, the root **run** does have a clear meaning, but the root **rupt** (from, for example, the words inter**rupt** and cor**rupt)**, does not. Can the group think of any affixes that could be attached to this root? Now pick an affix and see if it is one that can be joined to the root word. If it is, does the spelling of the root word need to change? Can the group explain the meaning of the new word? Can they explain the meaning of the affix?

Practise: Now, each pupil takes a turn to pick a lolly stick from each tray and decide if their suffix/prefix can be matched with their root word. They can consider what the newly built word means. Dictionaries or computers can be used to help clarify meanings and to check if the spelling of the root word needs to change at all.

Apply: When everyone has decided if their word parts match, they can form groups with those with the same prefix or suffix. Can they together come up with a definition of their affix? Can they write down any other words that could use that same affix?

Game 12: Morpheme Monsters

Summary

Pupils split words into morphemes – word roots and affixes. They then build new words and make sentences from them.

Resources

- A set of word cards for each pupil. Each word needs to include a different affix which could be interchanged with some or all of the other affixes to create new words.

- Two boxes, one labelled 'roots' and one labelled 'affixes'. These can be decorated as monsters.

- Scissors

- Dictionaries

- *Optional:* Some small rewards

Activity

Teach: Tell the group that you have two monsters who each like to eat different parts of words. Using some words other than those on your word cards to demonstrate, discuss what morphemes, root words and affixes are. Explain that one monster likes to eat root words and the other monster likes to eat affixes and that if you give them the wrong word part they get very angry. So you need help splitting up some words so that you can give your monsters the right food.

    Choose one of the words and, as a group, discuss if you can see a root word and an affix. Ask everyone to cut their word into two and to consider if the root word has a different spelling to its spelling when it's on its own. Now pupils feed their morphemes to the right monsters.

Practise: Choose another word card. Individually, pupils split their copy into a root and an affix. They take turns to feed their roots and affixes to the monsters (This can be hidden from the other children). If they give a monster a correct morpheme, they are rewarded (with a happy sigh?), but if it's wrong the monster shows its displeasure (a funny growl?).

    The group then discusses where the split was and considers if the root word's spelling was as it would be on its own, or different.

    Repeat with all the word cards.

Apply: Now each pupil can come and take one morpheme from each monster in order to build a new word. They can keep swapping their affixes and roots until they think they have two that can be joined. Having carefully looked at the two together, they feed them back to the monster and then go and write a sentence with the new word. Remind pupils that in some cases they may need to change the spelling of the root and that they can check in a dictionary if they wish.

Repeat until no more new words can be found.

Game 13: The Morpheme Meaning Matcher

Summary

Pupils match and examine words with the same affix and deduce the appropriate meaning for the affix. They then recall further words with this affix and consider how to spell them.

Resources

For each small group:

- Three sets of words, on individual word cards, each set using a specific prefix or suffix (see Appendix 2)
- Three different coloured sheets of A4 paper
- Definitions of the affixes used, each on a separate card, with a space to write in the affix
- Some blank word cards
- Glue sticks
- Dictionaries

Activity

Teach: Split into small groups to examine the word cards. As a large group, identify one set of words with the same suffix or prefix. Each small group sticks these onto one sheet of coloured paper. The large group reads and discusses the meanings of each word, considering how the affix affects the meanings. Dictionaries can be used as needed. Building on this analysis, select the appropriate definition for this affix and each small group adds the right definition card to their sheet, filling in the affix in the space provided.

Practise: In smaller groups, the pupils now group the other two sets of words with the same affixes. They discuss the meaning of the words, using dictionaries if needed, and select an appropriate definition for each affix. Groups compare their results.

Apply: Pupils now recall further words that use these affixes, writing them onto the blank word cards and adding them to the appropriate sheet. Who can write the sentence that contains the most words from one set?

Word association

Game 14: Silly Sentences

Summary

Pupils build silly or memorable sentences to associate words with the same grapheme–phoneme correspondences, root word or affix, to help them remember which words share a particular pattern.

Preparation

Select a set of words with a common pattern.

Resources

This game can be played without any pre-prepared resources. *Optional*:

- A set of words cards for each small group, each card containing one word from a set, *or*
- A set of blank word cards for each small group of pupils, for pupils to fill with each word from a set.

Activity

Teach: As a group, look at all the words in the set. Choose one word and read it out, identifying the separate graphemes and the phonemes they represent. Read through the other words. Highlight the common grapheme or sub-lexical unit and discuss the phoneme(s) it represents and letters it is built from. Can any other words with the same grapheme–phoneme correspondences be recalled? As a group, string together two or more of the words into a meaningful clause:

Jean was mean

Practise: In pairs, pupils add to this clause, changing it if they wish, to make a silly sentence or poem. Pupils share their efforts with the group. Write the favourite sentences on the board.

Jean was mean

When she beat Dean

At eating beans

If the sentence rhymes, any brave pupils can have a go at singing it!

Apply: Cover over any examples of words in the set and ask pupils to write down as many of these words as they can recall. Highlight again the common pattern. Can pupils write down a further word with this pattern?

Note: Examples of ready-made sentences for association can be found in Appendix 2. These can be used to support this game or to enhance other games by further associating the word sets being learnt.

Game 15: Perfect Pictures

Summary

Pupils design or find pictures that help to associate words with the same pattern.

Resources

- Drawing materials
- *Optional:* Internet access

Preparation

Select a set of words with a common pattern. Either choose a set that you have previously joined in a sentence (see Game 14) or a set that could be associated using pictures without the need for a sentence (see **ible** words below).

Activity

Teach: Show pupils a set of words, or a whole sentence that combines a set of words. Read the words or sentence and identify the common pattern. Focusing on each word in turn, carefully sound out the words and highlight the grapheme–phoneme correspondences. Discuss how the words or sentence could be illustrated with pictures. Search online for appropriate images, or sketch an image on the whiteboard.

Practise: Ask pupils to find or create better images. Share results and select some favourites.

The **creature** sold a **mixture** of **furniture** before his **departure** on an **adventure**

Is this you?

Terr **I** ble

incred **I** ble

Imposs **I** ble

sens **I** ble

Apply: Read the words again, this time with the new pictures to illustrate them. Further discuss the grapheme–phoneme correspondences and any tricky word parts. Put the words and pictures aside and ask pupils to write down as many of the words as they can remember.

Rules

Game 16: What's the Rule?

Summary

Pupils analyse a group of words that demonstrate a 'rule' in order to work out the rule, or guideline, for themselves.

Resources

- A group of words that demonstrate a guideline. (Colour, bold print, italics, font, font size and other formatting tools can be used to highlight particular aspects of a rule.)

  Example (for the guideline: *'When adding a suffix that begins with a vowel onto a word that ends with a silent **e**, then drop the silent **e**.'*):

fortun<u>e</u>, fortunate, desir<u>e</u>, desirable, lov<u>e</u>, lovable, lov<u>e</u>LESS

hop<u>e</u>, hoping, hop<u>e</u>FUL

To enhance word association, words can be brought together into sentences and illustrated with a picture:

*Although she was **fortunate** to have a **fortune**, she had a strong **desire** to be **desirable**. She wanted **love** but her life was **loveLESS**.*

Activity

Teach: Show the words or sentence to the pupils. Draw attention to the words that demonstrate the guideline.

Practise: Ask pupils to analyse the words in pairs and see if they can find a rule, or pattern, that the words are following. Feedback to the group and together finalise a perfect definition of the guideline.

Apply: Ask pupils to think of other examples of words that demonstrate the guideline.

Game 17: Building the Rules

Summary

Pupils develop and reinforce their understanding of a rule, or guideline, by choosing how to match word-part cards that demonstrate the pattern.

Resources

For each pupil:

- A set of word-part cards that demonstrate a guideline
- A dictionary

The examples below demonstrate the guideline: '*When adding a vowel suffix to a word ending in* **fer**, *double the* **r** *if the* **fer** *is stressed and don't double the* **r** *if the* **fer** *is not stressed*.'

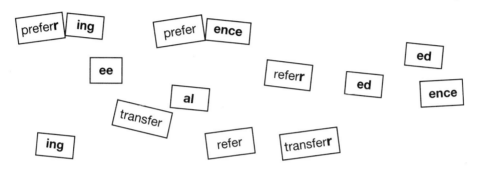

Activity

Teach: Select a couple of pairs of word-part cards to demonstrate the pattern (e.g. **prefer/ence** and **preferr/ing**). Ask if anyone knows for sure how to match up these pairs, or who can find out using a dictionary. Once the pairs have been correctly matched, ask if anyone can think of a pattern that explains why the words are matched in this way.

In this case, as with a number of patterns that depend on the *sounds* of word parts, a useful hint is to tell pupils to listen carefully to the sounds that the word parts are making and to exaggerate those sounds so that they can be clearly heard.

Practise: Once the guideline has been identified, ask pupils to match up the other word-part cards appropriately.

Apply: Tell pupils one or two other words that follow this guideline, where appropriate sounding them out carefully. Ask them to try and write down the words, using the guideline to help them spell the words correctly.

Tricky words

Game 18: Highlighter Heaven

Summary

Pupils identify the tricky part of a word, design related games and then choose the activity that will most help them to remember how to spell the word.

Resources

- Highlighter pens or pencils
- Paper or mini-whiteboards

Preparation

Select two words or sets of words that contain a tricky spelling pattern.

Activity

Teach: Tell the pupils one of the words. Sound it out carefully and ask pupils to try and write it down. Write the word on the board and ask everyone to highlight, on their own version, any parts that they found tricky. Compare which parts pupils found tricky and identify the most common parts:

P e o p l e

Now, as a group, consider silly or striking things that you could do to the word to make the spelling more memorable. You could:

- make a mnemonic
- make or find a picture. This could illustrate a mnemonic:

Peter eats other people's lovely eggs!!

or:

"O! What a big round tummy some pe ple have!"

- exaggerate or change the pronunciation of the word, for example, pronouncing it as it is spelt:

"pe o ple"

- make a silly sentence to emphasise the spelling:

Odd pe**o**ple **o**ften **o**gle **o**ranges.

- find words within words:

W**here** are we going?

<u>here</u>, t**here** and everyw**here**

- integrate the word into a picture to highlight a visual shape or pattern, e.g. the long 'y' and rounder 'e' in 'eye':

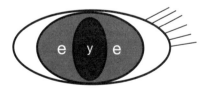

Practise: Ask everyone to select whichever version they think would most help them to remember the spelling. Hide all the versions of the word and ask everyone to try and spell the word again.

Now repeat the whole process with a different word, but this time ask pairs of pupils each to come up with something silly or striking to do with the word. Compare the different ideas and ask pupils to select and copy down their favourites.

Apply: Again hiding all versions of the word, ask pupils to try and write down both the words that you have practised.

Further multisensory approaches

Game 19: WordCraft

Summary

Pupils craft words out of various materials.

Resources

- A range of materials that can be moulded, twisted, bent, cut or placed into letter shapes, such as play dough, modelling clay, pipe cleaners, paper, card, felt, dried pasta or buttons
- Scissors

Preparation

- Select a set of words with a common pattern.

Activity

Teach: Select one word from your set. Say the word clearly and ask pupils to identify the first phoneme. Ask them to recall the grapheme that represents that phoneme. Can anyone draw it in the air? Discuss how to make this grapheme out of one of the materials. Shape it together. Repeat for each phoneme in the word, using a different material to mould each grapheme in order to demonstrate how the various materials can be manipulated.

Practise: Highlight to the pupils the pattern you are focusing on. Can they recall any other words that have this same pattern? Together, develop a verbal list of some other words in the pattern. Now, in pairs, pupils can choose one of these words to split into phonemes and then craft out of materials, grapheme by grapheme.

Can each pupil now work out what needs to stay and what to change if they want to craft a different word that has the same pattern?

Apply: As a group, look at all the words that have been made and think of a sentence using some of them. Ask pupils to write the sentence.

Game 20: Feel the Word

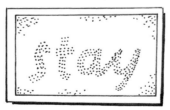

Summary

Pupils feel the pattern that a word makes through the tips of their fingers on rough materials of different textures, to aid future recall of the pattern.

Resources

- Each word in a set written in large, bold letters on a piece of A4 paper – one copy of each word for each pupil. *(Note: Cursive writing will create one flowing movement which some pupils will find easier to remember. However, this will not be useful for pupils who are not yet comfortable reading or writing cursive writing.)*
- Glue for each pupil
- Varied granular materials of different textures such as glitter, sand, sequins, lentils, rice

Activity

Teach: Take one of the words on an A4 sheet. As a group, discuss the word, pronouncing it carefully and identifying each grapheme–phoneme correspondence. Discuss and demonstrate how to paint glue onto the letters and then sprinkle with one of the granular materials, pouring away the excess.

Practise: Pupils choose a word, paint glue onto the letters and then cover with their preferred granular material. While this is drying, pupils repeat with one or two more words. When dry, pupils take a word and trace over the decorated letters with a finger, first with their eyes open and then with their eyes closed. Now pupils try to trace the word onto the table with their finger without looking at the decorated word. Repeat with the other words.

Apply: When pupils have successfully traced the word onto the table, they now write the word in correspondingly large letters onto paper with a big pen, again without looking at the decorated word. Following this, pupils can try to write the word with smaller handwriting.

Variation: Instead of initially tackling a whole word, first practise a common pattern, grapheme or tricky word-part with these sensory letters. Whole words can then be brought in at the 'Apply' stage.

Game 21: Big Word Play

Summary

Pupils use streamers, or another tool, to trace word parts, or whole words, with large full body movements. They then translate these movements into smaller fine motor movements.

Resources

- Tools for mark making or signalling with large body movements, such as:
  - streamers on sticks
  - mops, water and an outside concrete floor
  - chalks and a large chalkboard or appropriate floor
    or
  - whiteboard pens and a large whiteboard
- A3 paper and pens

Preparation

Select a grapheme or word part for pupils to learn.

Activity

Teach: Draw the grapheme in very large, bold letters on the board or floor. Say the sound, or sounds, that it represents. As a group, practise tracing or drawing the shape of the grapheme on the board or floor, or in the air, using the selected tools. Some pupils may benefit from tracing directly onto your drawn version or from having their arms guided by you. As they repeat the movement, pupils say the sound.

Practise: Pupils draw the grapheme, with slightly smaller movements, onto the A3 paper.

Apply: Tell the group a word that contains the grapheme or word part. If needed, write it for them to see and then take it away. Ask pupils to trace or draw the word with big movements, and then with slightly smaller movements onto the A3 paper. Can pupils now write the word with even smaller movements? Repeat with another word that contains the same word part.

Game 22: Mouth Awareness Game

Summary

Pupils explore the positions and movements of key articulators (e.g. lips, teeth, tongue) as they say a word and associate these movements with the appropriate phonemes and graphemes.

Resources

For each small group:

- A set of words for spelling, printed large onto a sheet. Start with a set in which all of the words are fairly short.

Activity

Teach: Select one word from the set. Tell the group that there are some humans stuck on another planet, who can read and write English but who don't know how to speak it. Explain that we can send these humans instructions for speaking in letters and emails, but not sound, so the group is going to write down for them instructions on how to say some words.

Now see how slowly the group can say the selected word. Focus on the first sound and discuss with the group what they do with their lips, teeth, tongue, jaw and breath to make this sound. When you have agreed on an instruction for the sound, look at the written word and ask the group to decide which grapheme or grapheme string the instruction covers. Now write the instruction on the whiteboard, clearly highlighting the grapheme that it refers to.

So, for the sound of **'p'** in the word **pain**, you might write:

For the 'p': Close your lips. Push them open with a short, quick breath.

Practise: Identify each of the further sounds in the word and identify the graphemes that represent them. Distribute these sounds between small groups and ask them to say the sound really slowly together and to discuss what their articulators are doing.

Come back as a group and complete the instructions. It can be fun to invite a guest into the classroom to try the instructions out on. Can the guest work out the word?

Apply: Choose another word in the set. Ask pupils to plan instructions for saying this word in small groups. When done, discuss and compare the instructions and write them up. Now, hiding the written instructions away, read out the instruction for one phoneme, leaving out which grapheme it relates to. See if pupils can first articulate the phoneme and then write down the grapheme that represents it. Try with other instructions.

Game 23: Hilarious Handwriting

Summary

Pupils attend closely to the sensation and movements of writing, with cursive handwriting, a word they are learning to spell, to aid recall. Paintbrush tickles create a high fun factor.

Resources

- A set of words displayed on the whiteboard
- Paint to share
- Paintbrushes and pens for each pupil

Activity

Teach: Choose two words from the set. If needed, help pupils to practise writing both words with cursive handwriting, either tracing or copying the written word. Now ask pupils to take a clean paintbrush and practise 'writing' one of the words slowly on the inside of their forearm, first with eyes open, if necessary looking at the written word, and then with eyes closed.

Practise: Now pupils gently and slowly trace the word they have been practising on a partner's forearm. Can their partner feel which of the two words they are writing? Is it the one that they have been practising themselves, or is it different?

Now make sure each pupil is matched with a partner who has been writing the same word. Can partners write the word on each other's forearm *in unison*, with their eyes closed?

Apply: With the word set no longer displayed, can pupils dip their brushes into paint and write the word on paper? Can they write it again with a pen?

Now further words in the set can be practised in the same way.

Revisiting and editing

These games help pupils to apply the spelling skills and knowledge taught and practised in previous games. Other games that work well for revisiting past spellings include those in the section 'Spoken words'.

Game 24: Who's This?

Summary

Pupils describe a character, using words in a word set just practised.

Resources

- A picture of an evocative or funny character, to which pupils could apply some words from a set of words recently practised.

  For example, a picture like the one below can be used following practice of words that use the grapheme **ou** for the /aʊ/ phoneme, such as *out*, *about*, *mouth*, *shout*, *sound*, *round* and *around*.

Activity

Teach: Show pupils the picture of a character. Together discuss who the character might be and how you could describe him or her.

Practise: Together recall words in the set of words that you have most recently been practising. With pupils, think of a sentence to describe the character using some of the words. Write it together on the board:

I saw a big, **round** monster when I was **out**.

Apply: Pupils add to this by writing further sentences of their own about the character, making sure that each sentence has at least one of the words from the set.

Variation: Ask pupils to find or draw a character of their own that they can describe with the words in a recently learnt word set.

Game 25: What Happened Next?

Summary

Pupils build a story together, ensuring that each paragraph uses at least one word from a set currently being practised.

Resources

- A first short paragraph of a story, including a word from the set of words currently being practised.

  For example, if you have been working on word endings with the spelling pattern **–cious**, such as *vicious*, *precious*, *conscious*, *delicious*, *malicious* and *suspicious*:

  Danny seemed to be making some silly mistakes in his recipes. Just today, his 'Supreme Chocolate Delight', which was usually delicious, tasted sour. Yesterday, his 'Incredible Crunchy Candy' had been soft. He was starting to get worried about his job as Master Sweetie Maker.

Activity

Teach: Read through the text. Ask pupils what they think the story is about and what might happen next. Ask if they can spot a word from the words you are currently practising and if they can remember any more words from the set. Who can remember how to spell the words?

Practise: Together, decide what might happen next and write on the board a few sentences to form the next section, making sure that one new word from the set is included.

Apply: Now tell pupils that they need to write a few more paragraphs to complete the story, each paragraph containing at least one word from the set. Read through some of the stories together. Compare which words from the set pupils have used and check how they have been spelt.

Game 26: Energetic Editing

Summary

Recently learnt words are written very fast and then pupils peer- or self-edit their work.

Resources

- A stopwatch, timer or clock with a second hand

Preparation

Have ready silly sentences for two sets of words recently learnt by the pupil group.

Activity

Teach: Discuss with pupils how they could tell if a word they have written might be spelt incorrectly and what they could do to try and correct it. Methods can include seeing if it looks 'right'; identifying the word parts, syllables or morphemes and seeing if each one looks 'right'; identifying the graphemes you've included in each word or word part and seeing if they match the phonemes you can hear in the spoken word or word part; recalling any other words in the same 'set' and remembering how they were spelt and also searching for the word in the dictionary.

Introduce a recently learnt set of words. Pupils call out the words in the set that they can remember and then recall or invent a silly sentence that includes as many of the words as possible. Pupils guess how quickly you can write the sentence on the board. With someone timing, write the sentence, purposefully making a number of mistakes. See how long it took and tell pupils that they can try and beat your time in a few minutes.

Practise: As a group, look for words that might be spelt incorrectly and underline them. Help the group to approach each of the underlined words with some of the editing methods listed above and to work out correct spellings.

Now score your joint editing work: 2 points for every correct original or edited word, 1 point for every correctly underlined but uncorrected or mis-corrected word, and 0 points for any unidentified mistakes.

Apply: Introduce another set of words recently practised and ask pupils to call out as many words in the set as they can and then to recall or invent a silly sentence that includes as many of the words as possible. Ask each pupil to write down the sentence as fast as they can, seeing how many can beat your time. Now ask pupils to carry out the editing process on their own work. Pairs can swap work for scoring. The winners are those with the highest score.

Variation: Instead of editing their own work, pupils can peer-edit. Pair pupils with others with similar spelling abilities. They swap their original written sentences in order to edit each other's. In this case, the score will apply to the scorer, not the original writer, as the score is for editing skills.

Game 27: Dashing Dictionary Delights!

Summary

Pupils use a dictionary to uncover mistakes in spellings or meanings.

Resources

For each pair:

- A dictionary
- A set of words with a common pattern, each on an individual card, one to include a spelling mistake
- A set of meanings on individual cards that match the words, one meaning to be incorrect
- *Optional:* An alphabetical order reminder card

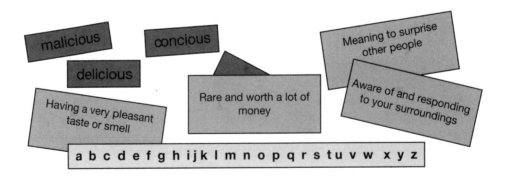

Activity

Teach: Choose a word from the set that has no mistakes in either its spelling or its meaning. Ask the whole group to check the spelling and meaning in their dictionary. If necessary, talk through how pupils can use knowledge of alphabetical order to find words.

Practise: Now explain that there are a total of two mistakes in the remaining words and meanings. Pairs use their dictionaries to find and correct the mistakes. Any pair who can find both mistakes inside a time limit set by you is a winner.

Apply: Which pair can write the most interesting paragraph that uses all of the words with their correct spellings and meanings?

8
Sample multi-activity spelling session

So far, we have looked at a wide range of strategies and individual activities that can help pupils to learn spellings. As teachers, we need to select from these to build complete spelling sessions that are multisensory and incorporate opportunities for us to teach and for pupils to practise and apply. We also need to structure each session within a cohesive series of sessions, allowing pupils to practise and recall words over time. Below is a sample outline for a multi-activity spelling session that includes ideas for homework and further follow-up sessions.

'ou' for the short /u/ sound

This sample session draws on Games 2, 9, 14, 15 and 24, as well as the Look Say Cover Write Check approach, and gives suggestions for further follow-up games.

Resources

- A large picture of two cheeky boys kicking footballs, the sentence, '*The couple of young cousins are double trouble*' partly visible, with blank footballs to be filled in with missing graphemes
- Handouts for each pupil with the same image
- Footballs – one for each pair of pupils

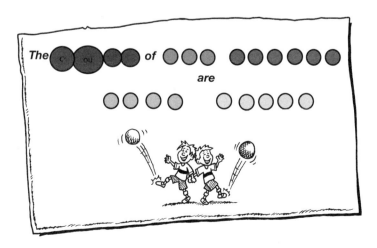

Activity

Teach: Introduce the large picture and say the silly sentence: '*The couple of young cousins are double trouble*'. See if anyone wants to try to rap or sing it.

Discuss the short /u/ sound. Ask if anyone can hear it in any of the words and discuss how it might be spelt. Introduce the grapheme **ou** for this sound. As a group, explore how to sound out each phoneme in the word **couple** and recall a grapheme for each phoneme. Fill in the graphemes on the picture. Identify and highlight any difficult graphemes.

Now, as a group, do the same for the words **young**, **cousins**, **double** and **trouble**.

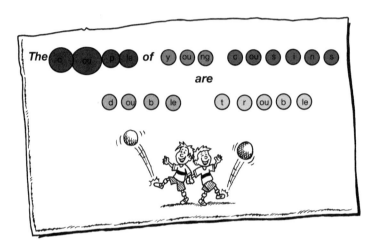

Practise: In pairs, pass a ball, spelling out one or two of the words, a grapheme at a time.

Apply: Now give each pupil a handout copy of the picture and see if they can fill in all of the footballs with the correct graphemes.

Homework activity

Ou for the short /u/ sound

1. *Read* the silly sentence.
2. *Say* the first word in the word column and the tip.
3. *Write* the word in the 'Write and Trace' column.
4. *Trace* over your written word with your finger or the end of a pen.
5. *Cover* up the word and try to write it again.
6. *Check* if it's right.
7. *Practise* again or repeat with the next word.

Silly Sentence

*The c**ou**ple of y**ou**ng c**ou**sins were d**ou**ble tr**ou**ble*

Word	Tip	Write and Trace	Try 1	Try 2
couple	c **ou** p le			
double	d **ou** b le			
trouble	t r **ou** b le			
cousins	c **ou** s i n s			
young	y **ou** ng			

> *Do you know any cheeky children? Write a short story about them. Use each word on the word list in a different sentence.*

_____

_____

_____

_____

_____

_____

_____

_____

_____

_____

Further follow-up activities

Following days can include games such as Grapheme Stick Man (Game 7) or Word Part Relay (Game 3) using this set of words split into graphemes in the same way. Later sessions can employ games from the 'Revisiting and editing' section.

9
Spelling at Home

There is ample evidence that family involvement has a significant impact on children's education. Drawing on a broad body of research, a 2008 report by the UK government found that: 'Parental behaviour has a bigger effect than school quality on pupils' attainment at Key stage 2' and that parental involvement in a child's education 'at age 7 independently predicted educational attainment at age 20' (Department for Children, Schools and Families, 2008).

Furthermore, as discussed, regular repetition and revisiting is a key tool to learning spelling. Spelling practice at home can be a vital component of a successful spelling programme. Most parents and other carers are keen to support their children's learning, but some lack the confidence, skills or knowledge to do so well. All parents can benefit from clear, straightforward guidance about the kind of help with spelling they can offer their children at home, particularly if we are sending home specific tasks to be undertaken there.

Look Say Cover Write Check tables are a useful resource for sending home, being reasonably straightforward to use and not requiring a very large time input. A number of the games described in this book can also be taken home for further practice. (For further guidance on this approach, see the Look Say Cover Write Check section of Chapter 2 Phonics Plus and also Chapter 8 Sample multi-activity spelling session.) Whatever is being sent home, accessible, straightforward instructions about the specific task need to be provided. In addition, a few points of general guidance can make a big difference. A brief introduction to phonemes, graphemes, word parts and affixes, along with some guidance about articulation, will support family members in successfully helping pupils to identify each of the distinct phonemes or longer word parts in a spoken word and to recall which grapheme represents them. A short session each year in school for parents and carers, or a standard leaflet home to each new parent group, can provide the information needed. It will also help if it is clear to parents and carers that they are always welcome to come in with questions or concerns about specific homework tasks or general spelling support.

Appendix 1: Some common affixes, their meanings and example words

Prefixes, meanings and examples

Prefix	Meaning	Example words
bi	two	bicycle, binoculars, binary
de	opposite, away from, down	detach, depart, depress
ex	out, out of, away from, lacking, former	extract, exhale, explode
mis	wrong	mistake, misuse, misspelling
non	not	nonsense, nonfiction
pre	before	prefix, predate, prepare, presume
re	again, back	return, reply, remake, revise
trans	move across or beyond	transport, transfer

Suffixes, meanings and examples

Suffix	Meaning	Example words
able	able to, having the quality of	adorable, tolerable, changeable, noticeable
er	someone who does	teacher, baker, painter, worker, farmer
er	comparative	bigger, taller, better
ible	having the quality of	sensible, terrible, horrible
ful	full of	wonderful, careful, playful, hopeful
less	without or lacking	joyless, hopeless, penniless, homeless
ment	the process or condition of	enjoyment, merriment, government
ness	in a state of	happiness, sadness, madness

Appendix 2: Word sets with activity suggestions

These tables provide sample spelling word sets, with corresponding sentences to aid learning. Some possible games from this book are also indicated. The word sets build on the spelling patterns listed in Appendix 1: Spelling of *The National Curriculum in England – English Programmes of Study: Key Stages 1 and 2.*

Shaded text is taken directly from the English Programme of Study (EPS). Text in *italics* indicates patterns and words that are statutory requirements of the EPS.

From Spelling – work for Year 1

Sample word set	From EPS Appendix 1. Statutory Requirement	From EPS Appendix 1. Rules and Guidance (non-statutory)	Some possible games	Example silly sentence / rhyme
off, cliff, cuff, fluff, daffodil, huff, gruff, puff, offer, puffin, stuff, sniff, stiff	*The sound /f/ spelt* **ff**	The /f/ sound is usually spelt as **ff** if it comes straight after a single vowel letter in short words. Exception: if	Game 2: Words on Pictures Game 20: Feel the Word	The pu**ff**in gave a sni**ff** At some flu**ff** on his cu**ff** Then a hu**ff** and a pu**ff** To blow the stu**ff** Down o**ff** the cli**ff**
bank, think, honk, chunk, bunk, blink, sank, sunk	*The /n/ sound spelt* **n** *before* **k**		Game 3: Word Part Relay Game 7: Grapheme Stick Man	I sat on the ba**nk** To have a thi**nk** And see the sun si**nk**. I gave a bli**nk** And the sun had su**nk**.
catch, fetch, kitchen, notch, hutch, hatch, snatch	**tch**	The /tʃ/ sound is usually spelt as **tch** if it comes straight after a single vowel letter. Exceptions: rich, which, much, such	Game 4: Treasure Hunt Game 8: We're Going on a Grapheme Hunt	Ca**tch** the cat! He's out of the ki**tch**en Into the hu**tch** To sna**tch** a rabbit For tea!
have, live, give, gave, love, dove, brave, cave, cove	*The /v/ sound at the end of words*	English words hardly ever end with the letter **v**, so if a word ends with a /v/ sound, the letter **e** usually needs to be added after the **v**.	Game 1: Grappling with Graphemes Game 21: Big Word Play	Ha**ve** you seen the bra**ve** do**ve** Who seems to li**ve** In the ca**ve** At the co**ve**?
rain, train, wait, afraid, paid	**ai**		Game 2: Words on Pictures Game 9: Catch	After we'd p**ai**d I'm afr**ai**d We had to w**ai**t In the r**ai**n For the tr**ai**n

From Spelling – work for Year 2

Sample word set	From EPS Appendix 1. Statutory Requirement	Rules and Guidance (non-statutory) English Programme of Study Appendix 1	Some possible games	Example silly sentence / rhyme
edge, bridge, badge, dodge, fudge	*The /dʒ/ sound spelt as **ge** and **dge** at the end of words, and sometimes spelt as **g** elsewhere in words before **e, i** and **y***	The letter **j** is never used for the /dʒ/ sound at the end of English words. At the end of a word, the /dʒ/ sound is spelt **dge** straight after the /æ/, /ɛ/, /ɪ/, /ɒ/, /ʌ/ and /ʊ/ sounds (sometimes called 'short' vowels). After all other sounds, whether vowels or consonants, the /dʒ/ sound is spelt as **ge** at the end of a word. In other positions in words, the /dʒ/ sound is often (but not always) spelt as **g** before **e, i,** and **y.** The /dʒ/ sound is always spelt as **j** before **a, o** and **u.**	Game 1: Grappling With Graphemes Game 6: Skittles	We sat at the e**dge** of a bri**dge** eating fu**dge**.
age, huge, change, charge, bulge, village			Game 2: Words on Pictures Game 15: Perfect Pictures	There's been a big chan**ge** since the hu**ge** bul**ge** made a char**ge** at our villa**ge**!
gem, giant, magic, giraffe, energy			Game 5: Kim's Game Game 14: Silly Sentences	The **gi**ant ma**gi**c **ge**m filled the **gi**raffe with ener**gy**.
jacket, jar, jog, join, just, jam, jaw, jump			Game 1: Grappling with Graphemes Game 21: Big Word Play	**J**ane **ju**mped over the **ja**m **ja**rs.

From Spelling – work for Years 3 and 4

Sample word set	From EPS Appendix 1. Statutory Requirement	Rules and Guidance (non-statutory) English Programme of Study Appendix 1	Some possible games	Example silly sentence / rhyme
double, trouble, country, cousin, couple	*The /ʌ/ sound spelt* **ou**		Game 5: Kim's Game Game 23: Hilarious Handwriting	The c**ou**ple of y**ou**ng c**ou**sins were d**ou**ble tr**ou**ble.
measure, treasure, pleasure, enclosure	*Words with endings sounding like / ʒə/ or /tʃə/*	The ending sounding like /ʒə/ is always spelt **sure**.	Game 4: Treasure Hunt Game 15: Perfect Pictures	It was a plea**sure** to mea**sure** all the trea**sure** in the enclo**sure**.
creature, adventure, furniture, mixture, departure		The ending sounding like /tʃə/ is often spelt **ture**, but check that the word is not a root word ending in (**t**)**ch** with an **er** ending – e.g. teacher, catcher, richer, stretcher	Game 3: Word Part Relay Game 14: Silly Sentences	The **creature** sold a **mixture** of **furniture** before his **departure** on an **adventure**.

From Word list – Years 3 and 4

Word	Sample word set	Possible games	Example silly sentence / rhyme / mnemonic
accident	accident, accelerate, access, accept, accident	Game 1: Grappling with Graphemes Game 9: Catch	If you **acc**elerate down a road with no **acc**ess you have to **acc**ept that you could have an **acc**ident.
arrive	arrange, arrest, arrive, arrow, arrogant	Game 5: Kim's Game Game 25: What Happened Next?	'We'll **arr**ange to **arr**est them as soon as they **arr**ive', said the police officer.
answer		Game 18: Highlighter Heaven	**A**dam **n**ever **s**miles **w**hen **e**ating **r**aspberries.

Sample word sets	From EPS Appendix 1. Statutory Requirement	Rules and Guidance (non-statutory)* English Programme of Study Appendix 1	Some possible games	Example silly sentence / rhyme
vicious, precious, conscious, delicious, malicious, suspicious	Endings which sound like /ʃəs/ spelt **cious** or **tious**	Not many common words end like this. If the root word ends in **ce**, the /ʃ/ sound is usually spelt as **c**.	Game 16: What's the Rule? Game 24: Who's This?	'How deli**cious**!' sneered the vi**cious** snake with a mali**cious** grin, after eating his pre**cious** prey.
ambitious, cautious, fictitious, infectious, nutritious		e.g. vice–vicious, grace–gracious, space–spacious, malice–malicious Exception: anxious	Game 11: Lucky Dip Game 27: Dashing Dictionary Delights!	Bob was cau**tious**. The plants looked nutri**tious** but could they give him an infec**tious** disease?
confidential, essential, partial, initial	Endings which sound like /ʃəl/	**cial** is common after a vowel letter and **tial** after a consonant letter, but there are some exceptions.	Game 4: Treasure Hunt Game 6: Skittles	It is essen**tial** that our ini**tial** meeting is confiden**tial**.
special, artificial, official, social		Exceptions: initial, financial, commercial, provincial (the spelling of the last three is clearly related to finance, commerce and province)	Game 14: Silly Sentences Game 23: Hilarious Handwriting	'The Best Artifi**cial** Flowers for all Spe**cial** So**cial** Occasions!!'

From Word list – Years 5 and 6

Word	Sample word set	Some possible games	Example silly sentence / rhyme / mnemonic
accommodate, accompany, according		Game 7: Grapheme Stick Man Game 18: Highlighter Heaven	**Acc**ording to zoo rules, parents must **acc**ompany children when near the zebra **acc**ommodation.
achieve	believe, brief, relief	Game 7: Grapheme Stick Man Game 9: Catch	'I bel**ieve** We can ach**ieve** Some rel**ief** From our gr**ief**!'
aggressive	progressive, expressive, passive, depressive, massive	Game 6: Skittles Game 25: What Happened Next?	'We're massive and progressive We're passive not aggressive We want to be expressive Not depressive Oh yeah!'

Glossary

Affix: A morpheme that is attached to a root word to form a new word.

Blend: To merge together individual phonemes to form a word.

Consonant cluster: A group of consonants that have no intervening vowels, e.g. **spl**.

Consonant: A sound which is produced when the speaker closes off or obstructs the flow of air through the vocal tract, usually using lips, tongue or teeth. Most of the letters of the alphabet represent consonants. Only the letters **a**, **e**, **i**, **o**, **u** and **y** can represent vowel sounds.

Digraph: A grapheme with two letters representing one phoneme. Sometimes, these two letters are not next to one another; this is called a *split digraph*, e.g. l**a**n**e**.

Etymology: The study of the origin of words and the way in which their *meanings* and forms have changed throughout history.

Grapheme: The single letter, or the group of letters, that we use to represent each phoneme.

Grapheme–phoneme correspondence (GPC): The link between graphemes and the phonemes that they represent. In the English writing system, a grapheme may correspond to more than one phoneme.

Homophone: A word that is pronounced the same as another word but differs in meaning, and may differ in spelling, e.g. **there**, **their** and **they're**.

Morpheme: The smallest unit of meaning in a language.

Morphology: The study of a language's morphemes and other linguistic units.

Phoneme: A distinct unit of sound, e.g. the **'sh'** sound in the spoken word **'fish'**.

Phonics: The method for teaching reading and writing by developing pupils' ability to hear, identify, and manipulate phonemes, in order to teach the correspondence between phonemes and the spelling patterns (graphemes) that represent them.

Prefix: An affix placed at the beginning of a word.

Root word: A word without any affixes.

Schwa: The phoneme represented as /ə/ in the International Phonetic Alphabet. The phoneme represented by the grapheme **er** in the word sist**er**.

Segment(ation): To split a word into individual phonemes.

Semantics: The study of meaning in words, phrases, sentences, and larger units of discourse.

Sub-lexical: Referring to a word part. Commonly used in relation to word parts that are smaller than a whole word and larger than a single phoneme or grapheme.

Suffix: An affix placed at the end of a word.

Syntax: The set of rules, principles and processes that govern the structure of sentences in a given language.

Vowel: A speech sound that comes from the lungs, through the vocal cords, and is not blocked, so there is no friction. Also the letters in the alphabet that represent these sounds. The letters in English that are vowels are: **a**, **e**, **i**, **o**, **u** and sometimes **y**.

Bibliography

Berninger, V. (2012) 'Evidence-Based, Developmentally Appropriate Writing Skills K to 5: Teaching the Orthographic Loop of Working Memory to Write Letters So Developing Writers Can Spell Words and Express Ideas'. Presented at Handwriting in the 21st Century? An Educational Summit. Washington, DC, January 23, 2012. Available online at: www.hw21summit.com/media/zb/hw21/H2937N_Berninger_presentation.pdf (accessed 20/5/15).

Bosman, A. and Orden, V. (1997) 'Why spelling is more difficult than reading' in C.A. Perfetti, L. Rieben and M. Fayol (eds), *Learning to Spell: Research, Theory and Practice across Languages*. Jillsdale, NJ: Lawrence Erlbaum Associates. Chapter available online at: http://xn--awww-9na2499b.annabosman.eu/documents/BosmanVanOrden1997b.pdf (accessed 3/3/15).

Chomsky, N. (1975) *Reflections on Language*. New York: Pantheon Books.

Clark, R.E., Kirschner, P.A. and Sweller, J. (2012) 'Putting students on the path to learning: The case for fully guided instruction'. *American Educator*, Spring 2012. Available online at www.aft.org/sites/default/files/periodicals/Clark.pdf (accessed 7/7/15).

Coffield, F., Moseley, D., Hall, E. and Ecclestone, K. (2004) *Learning Styles and Pedagogy in Post-16 Learning. A Systematic and Critical Review*. London: Learning and Skills Research Centre.

Cook, L. (2011) *Effects of Multisensory Instruction on Spelling in Second Grade*. Appalachian State University. Available online at www.ltl.appstate.edu/ . . . /Research-paper-effects-of-multisensory-instruction-on-spelling.doc (accessed 5/3/15).

Crystal, D. (2003) *The Cambridge Encyclopedia of the English Language* (2nd edn). Cambridge: Cambridge University Press.

Department for Children School and Families (2008) *The Impact of Parental Involvement on Children's Education*.

Department for Education (2013) *English Programmes of Study: Key Stages 1 and 2; The National Curriculum in England*.

Ehri, L., Nunes S., Stahl S. and Willows, D. (2001) 'Systematic phonics instruction helps students learn to read: Evidence from National Reading Panel's meta-analysis'. *Review of Educational Research*, Fall 2001, vol. 71, (3), 393–447.

Fisher, B., Cozens, M.E. and Greive, C. (2007) 'Look-Say-Cover-Write-Say-Check and Old Way/New Way – mediational learning: a comparison of the effectiveness of two tutoring programs for children with persistent spelling difficulties'. *Education Papers and Journal Articles*, Paper 31. School of Education at ResearchOnline@Avondale. Available online at http://research.avondale.edu.au/edu_papers/31 (accessed 30/3/15).

Frith, U. (1985) 'Beneath the surface of developmental dyslexia' in J.C. Marshall, K.F. Patterson and M. Coltheart (eds), *Surface Dyslexia in Adults and Children*. London: Routledge and Kegan Paul. Available online at www.icn.ucl.ac.uk/dev_group/ufrith/documents/Frith,%20Beneath%20the%20surface%20of%20developmental%20dyslexia%20copy.pdf (accessed 14/6/15).

Gentry, J.R. (2011a) 'Teaching spelling in the 21st century'. Keystone handout. Available online at http://jrichardgentry.com/Keystone%20Handout%20102511.pdf (accessed 15/5/15).

Gentry, J.R. (2011b) 'Raising readers, writers, and spellers'. Blog in *Psychology Today*. Available at https://www.psychologytoday.com/blog/raising-readers-writers-and-spellers/201103/fail-fails-our-children-no-more-spelling-tests (accessed 28 July 2015).

Jaspers, K.E., Williams, R.L., Skinner, C.H., Cihak, D., McCallum, R.S. and Ciancio, D.J. (2012) 'How and to what extent do two cover, copy, and compare spelling interventions contribute to spelling, word recognition, and vocabulary development?' *Journal of Behavioral Education*, vol. 21, 20–98.

Hepplewhite, D. (2011) 'Children not segmenting as expected'. Online forum discussion at Debbie Hepplewhite's SyntheticPhonics.com. Available at www.syntheticphonics.com/message/viewtopic.php?t=474&sid=3877e5117 7c454a86178efbfedf70ae1 (accessed 4/3/15).

Horobin, S. (2013) 'Does spelling matter?' Online article on Oxford Dictionaries' OxfordWords blog available at: http://blog.oxforddictionaries.com/2013/04/does-spelling-matter/ (accessed 21/2/15).

Jensen, E. (2005) *Teaching with the Brain in Mind* (2nd edn). Alexandria, VA: Association for Supervision and Curriculum Development.

Jolliffe, W., Waugh, D. and Carss, A. (2012) *Teaching Systematic Synthetic Phonics in Primary Schools.* London: Sage Publications Ltd.

Kelly, K. and Phillips, S. (2011) *Teaching Literacy to Learners with Dyslexia: A Multi-Sensory Approach.* London: Sage.

Kolb, D. A. (1984) *Experiential Learning: Experience as the Source of Learning and Development.* Englewood Cliffs, NJ: Prentice Hall.

Mann, T.B., Bushell, D. and Morris, E.K. (2010) 'Use of sounding out to improve spelling in young children'. *Journal of Applied Behaviour Analysis*, 43, (1), 89–93.

Michael, J. (2006) 'Where's the evidence that active learning works?'. *Advances in Physiology Education*, 30 (4), 159–67.

Montgomery, D. (2012) 'The contribution of handwriting and spelling remediation to overcoming dyslexia', in T. Wydell and L. Fern-Pollack (eds), *Dyslexia: A Comprehensive and International Approach* (pp. 109–46). intechopen.com.

Nunes, T. and Bryant, P. (2006) *Improving Literacy by Teaching Morphemes.* London: Routledge.

Nunes, T., Bryant, P. and Barros, R. (2012) 'The development of word recognition and its significance for comprehension and fluency'. *Journal of Educational Psychology*, vol. 104, (4).

Pashler, H., McDaniel, M., Rohrer, D. and Bjork, R. (2008) 'Learning styles: concepts and evidence'. *Psychological Science in the Public Interest*, vol. 9, (3), 105–19.

Phillips, S., Kelly, K. and Symes, L. (2013) *Assessment of Learners with Dyslexic-Type Difficulties.* London: Sage.

Phillips, W.E. and Feng, J. (2012) 'Methods for sight word recognition in kindergarten: traditional flashcard method vs. multisensory approach'. Paper presented at the 2012 Annual Conference of Georgia Educational Research Association, October 18–20, 2012. Savannah, Georgia. Available online at http://files.eric.ed.gov/fulltext/ED536732.pdf (accessed 5/5/2015).

Piaget, J. (1955) *The Language and Thought of the Child.* New York: The New American Library.

Prince, M. (2004) 'Does active learning work? A review of the research'. *Journal of Engineering Education*, vol. 93, issue 3.

Rose, J. (2006) *Independent Review of the Teaching of Early Reading.* Department for Education and Skills.

Rosen, M. and Oxenbury, H. (1989) *We're Going on A Bear Hunt.* London: Walker Books.

Shlagal, B. (1998) 'American spelling instruction: what history tells us'. Online article on the American Reading Forum website. Available at http://americanreadingforum.org/yearbook/yearbooks/98_yearbook/pdf/02_schlagal_98.pdf (accessed 10/7/15).

Shams, L. and Seitz A. (2008) 'Benefits of multisensory learning', in *Trends in Cognitive Sciences*. University of California Riverside. Available at http://faculty.ucr.edu/~aseitz/pubs/Shams_Seitz08.pdf (accesssed 30/4/15).

Shoval, E. (2011) 'Using mindful movement in cooperative learning while learning about angles'. *Instructional Science*, vol. 39, issue 4, 453–66.

Smith, F. (1994) *Writing and the Writer.* Hillsdale, NJ: Lawrence Erlbaum Associates.

Stahl, S. A. (2002). 'Different strokes for different folks?', in L. Abbeduto (ed.), *Taking Sides: Clashing on Controversial Issues in Educational Psychology* (pp. 98–107). Guilford, CT, USA: McGraw-Hill.

Stansfield, J. (2012) *Dyslexia: Early Identification.* British Dyslexia Association.

StudentGems (2012) 'Standing out from the crowd'. Online article on the StudentGems blog. Available at http://blog.studentgems.com/2012_03_01_archive.html (accessed 10/7/15).

Vygotsky, L. (1978) *Mind in Society: the Development of Higher Psychological Processes.* New York: Harvard University Press.

Waugh, D., Warner, C. and Waugh, R. (2013) *Teaching Grammar, Punctuation and Spelling in Primary Schools.* London: Sage Publications Ltd.

Westwood, P. (2014) *Teaching Spelling: Exploring Common Sense Strategies and Best Practices.* Oxon: Routledge.